Southern Living.

The
SOUTHERN
HERITAGE
COOKBOOK
LIBRARY

The SOUTHERN HERITAGE
Just Desserts
COOKBOOK

OXMOOR HOUSE
Birmingham, Alabama

Southern Living

The Southern Heritage Cookbook Library

Copyright 1984 by Oxmoor House, Inc.
Book Division of Southern Progress Corporation
P.O. Box 2262, Birmingham, Alabama 35201

Southern Living® is a federally registered trademark belonging to
Southern Living, Inc.

Library of Congress Catalog Number: 83-082156
ISBN: 0-8487-0606-4

Manufactured in the United States of America

The Southern Heritage JUST DESSERTS Cookbook

Manager, Editorial Projects: Ann H. Harvey
Southern Living® *Foods Editor*: Jean W. Liles
Production Editor: Joan E. Denman
Foods Editor: Katherine M. Eakin
Director, Test Kitchen: Laura N. Massey
Test Kitchen Home Economists: Kay E. Clarke, Rebecca J. Riddle,
    Elizabeth J. Taliaferro, Dee Waller
Production Manager: Jerry R. Higdon
Copy Editor: Melinda E. West
Editorial Assistants: Patty E. Howdon, Mary Ann Laurens,
    Karen P. Traccarella
Food Photographer: Jim Bathie
Food Stylist: Sara Jane Ball
Layout Designer: Christian von Rosenvinge
Mechanical Artist: Faith Nance
Research Editors: Evelyn deFrees, Alicia Hathaway

Special Consultants

Art Director: Irwin Glusker
Heritage Consultant: Meryle Evans
Foods Writer: Lillian B. Marshall
Food and Recipe Consultants: Marilyn Wyrick Ingram,
    Audrey P. Stehle

Cover (clockwise from bottom): Fresh Peach Meringues (page 117),
Crème de Menthe Parfaits (page 103), Strawberry Charlotte (page 84),
Chocolate-Filled Cream Puffs Deluxe (page 122), Mocha Ice Cream Roll
(page 102). Photograph by Jim Bathie.

Harris County Heritage Society

CONTENTS

An elegant array of desserts (clockwise from front):
Wine Jelly Mold (page 70), Honey Flummery (page 75),
Charlotte Russe (page 82), Rose Hill Strawberries
(page 33), Ambrosia (page 30), Blitz Torte
(page 126), and Opa's Torte (page 125).

INTRODUCTION

It would be impossible to overstate the importance of sweets to a Southerner. It is likely that the most rabid sweet-cravers among us trace our lineage back to the English, whose sweet-eating, in the opinion of the French, amounted to a mindless addiction: They even put sugar into their wine! Queen Elizabeth herself kept a "sucket," later called a sweetmeat, in her mouth most of the time.

The seventeenth-century dining table was set flat with food dishes edge to edge, matched cross-corner, and side to side. No centerpiece was used except an odd-shaped dish as part of the design. The standard two-course dinner permitted sweet dishes to be placed among the meats and vegetables; fruit and nuts alone were reserved for "dessert."

By the mid-1700s, the dessert tables of Kings were being eyed by the American gentry, and tureens and footed salvers called "middle stands" began arriving. George Washington ordered such a stand in 1760. With elevation came revelation; enter the dessert table, separate and complete with centerpiece, a landscape of highs and lows. Desserts reached ever upward as glass, silver, and porcelain makers came out with pyramids of graduated salvers, epergnes, and that Everest of centerpieces, the pineapple stand.

The display was a statement of the hostess' brilliance and imagination; she might place her dessert table behind a curtain or at the head of a stairway for dramatic effect. And if her bright red dessert jelly tasted of beets or her green of spinach, diarists of the day apparently did not comment on it. Or she might engage the services of a confectioner such as Frederick Kreitner, a Charlestonian, who lodged this notice in the *American General Gazette* in 1777: "The Subscriber . . . makes Figures suitable for Desart Tables, Fountains, Landscapes, Scripture and Ovidie Pieces, in the Italian Manner, done on the shortest Notice, and at the Cheapest Rates. . . ."

While wealthy planters and affluent merchants along the coast could afford such indulgence, the vast majority of the population was more familiar with rice or bread pudding, apple and sweet potato desserts, using more molasses than sugar. This book looks at — and celebrates — both extremes and all the delicious sweets in the middle.

THE PROOF OF THE PUDDING

I n the beginning, there was porridge. Thinner, it was gruel; thicker, it was bread. Long before it became Scandinavian Creamy, it was everyday grain boiled in water and seasoned with a little salt, and it was the staff of life. Only the grain differed from one country to another. When honey was found, people sweetened their porridge; they added milk when they had it and otherwise improved upon a good thing.

With experimentation, there came pudding-on-purpose: Sweetened bready mixtures such as "plum" pudding were boiled in a dampened, flour-rubbed cloth. With iron hearthware, it became possible to bake puddings long before ovens came into general use. Some of those baked puddings found their way into crusts and became pies.

Mary Randolph's *The Virginia Housewife*, 1824, demonstrated how peaceably the English plum pudding, sweetened with sugar, co-existed with Indian pudding, sweetened with molasses. Cornmeal mush, leftover cornbread, and biscuits all enjoyed an afterlife as puddings. New Orleans French bread makes an exceptionally fine one as exemplified in the bread pudding served by Bon Ton, the famed New Orleans restaurant. Rice pudding gained a following in the South, except in the Low Country of the Carolinas, where "sweet" rice is still regarded by some as a form of poison. The Queen of Puddings, when adopted by the French, became *La Reine des Poudings*, but when they got it from the English, there was no French word for pudding; they just modified the spelling and kept the traditional dessert.

The nineteenth century saw an explosion of improvements in kitchen furnishings and in the availability of ingredients. By 1900, the cook had access to fine sugar and cast iron stoves, refined flour and her choice of many models of apple parers. Tapioca, made of the bitter cassava root, came from the West Indies . . . another starch to thicken her puddings. Moreover, with every advance in food technology, the housewife baked better bread, the foundation of some of grandmother's best desserts.

Queen of Puddings (center) baked in individual cups, Rice Pudding with Currants (left), and Bread Pudding with Lemon Sauce, all shown in the Preparation Room of the restored Tryon Palace, New Bern, North Carolina.

BACK TO BASICS

SCANDINAVIAN CREAMY PORRIDGE

1½ cups whipping cream
1 cup all-purpose flour
3 cups milk, scalded
2 tablespoons sugar
½ teaspoon salt
¼ teaspoon ground cinnamon
Additional ground cinnamon
  (optional)

Place whipping cream in top of a double boiler. Cook over boiling water 10 minutes, stirring constantly. Add flour, stirring with a wire whisk until smooth. Gradually add scalded milk, stirring until smooth. Stir in sugar, salt, and ¼ teaspoon cinnamon. Cook over low heat 10 minutes, stirring frequently. Spoon into individual serving bowls, and sprinkle with additional cinnamon, if desired. Serve hot. Yield: about 4½ cups.

HASTY PUDDING

½ cup butter or margarine
½ cup all-purpose flour
3 cups milk
1 teaspoon ground
  nutmeg
¾ cup sugar
1 tablespoon ground
  cinnamon
3 tablespoons butter or
  margarine

Melt ½ cup butter in a heavy saucepan over low heat; add flour, stirring until smooth. Cook 1 minute, stirring constantly. Gradually add milk; cook over medium heat, stirring constantly, until thickened and bubbly. Stir in nutmeg.
Pour milk mixture into a greased 1-quart casserole. Combine sugar and cinnamon; sprinkle sugar mixture evenly over milk mixture. Dot with butter. Broil 6 inches from heating element 8 minutes or until butter melts and pudding is lightly browned. Spoon into individual serving bowls. Serve hot or cold. Yield: 4 to 6 servings.

Photographer: Mary-Gray Hunter

Hasty Pudding. How can something so simple taste so good?

Hasty Pudding is an old-time staple British porridge. By tradition, it was made of oatmeal or wheat flour and water. But after transplanting himself to America, the Englishman found corn instead of the accustomed grains, and his Hasty Pudding, made with flour and sugar, became Indian Pudding, made with cornmeal and molasses. Cornmeal was frequently referred to by the settlers as "Indian" or "Injun."

INDIAN PUDDING

4 cups milk
⅓ cup molasses
½ cup yellow cornmeal
¼ cup sugar
½ teaspoon ground
   ginger
¼ teaspoon salt

Combine milk and molasses in a saucepan; mix well. Add remaining ingredients. Cook over medium heat, stirring constantly, 10 minutes or until thickened.

Pour pudding into a greased 1-quart casserole. Bake, uncovered, at 300° for 1 hour. Spoon into serving bowls; serve hot. Yield: 6 to 8 servings.

Note: Traditionally, Indian Pudding bakes for several hours. Baking time for this recipe has been decreased to meet today's more efficient standards of food preparation.

MUSH PUDDING

2 cups boiling water
½ cup yellow cornmeal
¼ cup cold water
½ teaspoon salt
3 eggs, beaten
1 cup milk
1½ cups sugar
1 tablespoon butter or
   margarine, softened
Lemon sauce (pages 136-37)

Pour boiling water into top of a double boiler; stir in cornmeal, water, and salt. Cook over boiling water, stirring occasionally, 2 to 3 minutes; cool.

Stir cornmeal mixture into eggs in a large bowl. Add remaining ingredients; mix well.

Pour mixture into a well-greased 13- x 9- x 2-inch baking pan. Bake, uncovered, at 250° for 2 hours and 15 minutes. Serve warm with lemon sauce. Yield: 8 servings.

Illustration from Joel Barlow's The Hasty Pudding, *1796.*

WW I food conservation display.

BON TON'S BREAD PUDDING

1 (16-ounce) loaf French
   bread, cut into 1-inch cubes
4 cups milk
3 eggs, beaten
2 cups sugar
1 cup raisins
3 tablespoons butter or
   margarine, melted
2 tablespoons vanilla extract
Whiskey Sauce

Combine bread and milk in a large mixing bowl; set aside 5 minutes. Add eggs, sugar, raisins, butter, and vanilla; stir well. Spoon mixture into a greased 3-quart casserole. Bake, uncovered, at 325° for 1 hour or until firm. Cool in pan at least 20 minutes before serving. Spoon into individual serving bowls; serve with Whiskey Sauce. Yield: 8 to 10 servings.

Whiskey Sauce:

½ cup butter or margarine,
   softened
1 cup sugar
1 egg, beaten
1 tablespoon bourbon

Combine butter and sugar in a small saucepan; cook over medium heat, stirring frequently, until sugar dissolves. Add egg, stirring briskly with a wire whisk until well blended. Cook over medium heat 1 minute. Remove from heat, and let cool completely. Stir in bourbon. Yield: about 1¼ cups.

New Orleans' Bon Ton Restaurant is one of the favorite haunts of the young business set. It caught on quickly when Acadian Al Pierce opened it in 1953 and continues to flourish, led by his nephew and his wife, Debbie. The ambience may be described as bustling, cheery, and crowded. Worth saving room for is the Cajun-style bread pudding.

Still Life with Bread Box,
oil on canvas by
Sylvia Alberts, 1979.

THE UNIFORM BREAD SLICER

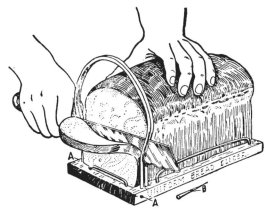

BREAD PUDDING WITH LEMON SAUCE

3 tablespoons butter or
  margarine, softened
4 slices bread
4 eggs
½ cup sugar
2 cups milk, scalded
½ cup golden raisins
2 tablespoons butter or
  margarine
1 teaspoon vanilla extract
Lemon Sauce

Spread 3 tablespoons butter on bread slices. Trim and discard crust; cut slices into cubes.

Beat eggs in a large bowl; stir in bread, sugar, milk, raisins, 2 tablespoons butter, and vanilla. Pour into a greased 1½-quart casserole. Place casserole in a pan of warm water. Bake at 300° for 50 minutes or until a knife inserted in center comes out clean. Cool; serve with Lemon Sauce. Yield: 6 servings.

Lemon Sauce:

4 egg yolks, beaten
½ cup sugar
¼ cup flour
1½ cups milk, scalded
¼ cup lemon juice

Combine yolks, sugar, flour, and milk in a saucepan; mix well. Cook over medium heat, stirring constantly, until thickened. Remove from heat, and stir in lemon juice. Serve hot. Yield: 2 cups.

BREAD PUDDING WITH WINE SAUCE

8 slices bread
3 cups milk
3 eggs, beaten
½ cup sugar
2 tablespoons butter or
  margarine, melted
1 teaspoon vanilla extract
⅛ teaspoon salt
½ cup raisins
Grape Wine Sauce

Soak bread in milk in a large mixing bowl 10 minutes. Place bread in a well-greased 2-quart casserole, and set aside. Reserve milk in mixing bowl.

Add eggs, sugar, butter, vanilla, salt, and raisins to reserved milk; beat well. Pour over bread in casserole. Bake, uncovered, at 325° for 1 hour. Spoon into individual serving dishes, and serve hot or at room temperature with Grape Wine Sauce. Yield: 8 servings.

Grape Wine Sauce:

¾ cup water
¼ cup sugar
1½ tablespoons cornstarch
½ cup sweet red wine

Combine water, sugar, and cornstarch in a medium saucepan. Cook over medium-high heat, stirring constantly, until clear and thickened; stir in wine. Reduce heat to medium; cook until well blended. Serve hot. Yield: about 1 cup.

CARAMEL BREAD PUDDING

½ cup sugar
3 cups milk, scalded
2 cups soft breadcrumbs
2 eggs, beaten
¼ teaspoon salt
¼ teaspoon ground nutmeg
3 tablespoons butter or
  margarine, melted
¾ teaspoon vanilla extract
Sweetened whipped cream

Place sugar in a 9-inch cast-iron skillet; cook over medium heat, stirring constantly with a wooden spoon, until sugar dissolves and becomes a golden syrup. Gradually pour syrup into milk in a large mixing bowl, beating constantly, until syrup dissolves in milk. Stir in breadcrumbs, eggs, salt, nutmeg, butter, and vanilla.

Pour mixture into a greased 1½-quart casserole. Place casserole in a 13- x 9- x 2-inch baking pan; pour hot water into pan to a depth of ½ inch. Bake, uncovered, at 350° for 1 hour or until lightly browned. Spoon into individual serving bowls, and serve warm with sweetened whipped cream. Yield: 6 to 8 servings.

QUEEN OF PUDDINGS

3 cups milk
2 eggs, separated
1 tablespoon butter or
  margarine
1 teaspoon grated lemon
  rind
1 teaspoon vanilla extract
⅛ teaspoon salt
1½ cups graham cracker
  crumbs
¾ cup sugar, divided
½ cup red currant jelly

Combine milk, egg yolks, butter, lemon rind, vanilla, and salt in a medium saucepan; mix well. Place over medium heat and cook, stirring constantly, until thoroughly heated (mixture will not thicken). Remove from heat.

Combine cracker crumbs and ½ cup sugar; fold into milk mixture. Spoon mixture into six 6-ounce lightly greased custard cups. Place cups in a 13- x 9- x 2-inch baking pan; add hot water to a depth of 1 inch. Bake at 325° for 35 minutes or until a knife inserted in center comes out clean. Remove from oven, and set aside to cool slightly.

Slightly soften jelly in a small saucepan over low heat. Spread jelly over top of each individual pudding.

Beat egg whites (at room temperature) until foamy. Add remaining sugar, 1 tablespoon at a time, beating until soft peaks form. Fill a pastry bag with meringue; pipe onto center of each pudding.

Bake at 425° for 6 minutes or until meringue is lightly browned. Serve immediately. Yield: 6 servings.

Arkansas Rice Pudding: It is the chewy coconut topping that sets this one apart from the rest.

ARKANSAS RICE PUDDING

¼ cup butter or margarine
3 eggs
1 cup sugar
3 cups milk
2½ cups cooked regular rice,
  cooled
2 teaspoons vanilla extract
¾ teaspoon ground nutmeg
½ teaspoon salt
¾ cup grated coconut

Preheat oven to 325°. Place ¼ cup butter in a 12- x 8- x 2-inch baking dish. Place baking dish in oven, and heat until butter melts. Remove from oven, and set aside.

Beat eggs in a large bowl; gradually add sugar, beating well. Stir in milk, rice, vanilla, nutmeg, and salt. Pour into baking dish; sprinkle coconut over top. Bake, uncovered, at 325° for 1 hour. Spoon into individual serving bowls; serve hot. Yield: 10 servings.

Shipping the Crop, an 1876 color engraving of rice being loaded in Louisiana.

NORWEGIAN RICE PUDDING

4 cups water
2 cups milk
1 cup regular rice, uncooked
½ cup sugar
½ teaspoon salt
1 cup whipping cream
1 (8¼-ounce) can crushed pineapple, drained
1 (6-ounce) jar maraschino cherries, drained and halved
1 teaspoon vanilla extract

Bring water to a boil in a large saucepan; stir in milk, rice, sugar, and salt. Reduce heat to low; cover and cook 1 hour (do not allow to boil), stirring twice. Remove from heat; allow to cool to room temperature. Cover and refrigerate overnight.

Beat whipping cream in a large mixing bowl until soft peaks form. Fold in pineapple, cherries, vanilla, and cold rice mixture. Spoon into individual serving bowls, and serve chilled. Yield: 8 to 10 servings.

RICE PUDDING WITH CURRANTS

3 cups cooked regular rice
3 cups milk
2 tablespoons butter or margarine
2 eggs, beaten
½ cup sugar
½ teaspoon ground cinnamon
¾ cup currants
½ teaspoon vanilla extract

Combine rice, milk, and butter in a large saucepan. Stir in eggs. Combine sugar and cinnamon, stirring until well blended. Add sugar mixture to rice mixture. Cook over medium heat, stirring constantly, 20 minutes or until liquid is absorbed.

Stir in currants and vanilla. Cool slightly. Spoon into a large serving bowl. Serve warm or cold. Yield: 12 servings.

BAKED RICE PUDDING

1 cup sugar
1½ teaspoons cornstarch
⅛ teaspoon ground nutmeg
3 eggs, beaten
2 cups milk
1 cup raisins
⅔ cup cooked regular rice
½ teaspoon vanilla extract

Combine sugar, cornstarch, and nutmeg in a medium mixing bowl; add eggs, beating until well combined. Add milk, raisins, rice, and vanilla, stirring well. Pour mixture into a greased 8-inch square pan. Place prepared pan in a 13- x 9- x 2-inch baking pan; add boiling water to a depth of 1 inch.

Bake at 325° for 1 hour or until a knife inserted in center comes out clean. Spoon into individual serving bowls. Serve hot. Yield: 6 to 8 servings.

Note: This is a good recipe for using leftover rice.

Peppermint Tapioca Pudding: Make it special with Whipped Cream-Chocolate Sauce.

PEPPERMINT TAPIOCA PUDDING

3 eggs, separated
4 cups milk
1 cup crushed peppermint
  candy
¼ cup sugar
¼ cup instant tapioca
¼ teaspoon salt
Whipped Cream-Chocolate
  Sauce
Additional crushed
  peppermint candy

Combine egg yolks and next 5 ingredients in top of a double boiler; beat well. Cook over boiling water, stirring frequently, 20 minutes or until mixture is thickened; let cool completely.

Beat egg whites (at room temperature) until soft peaks form. Fold into tapioca mixture. Cover; chill several hours or overnight.

Spoon a heaping ½ cupful of peppermint tapioca into each of twelve 5-ounce parfait glasses. Top each with 3 tablespoons Whipped Cream-Chocolate Sauce. Sprinkle crushed peppermint candy over each pudding. Yield: 12 servings.

Whipped Cream-Chocolate Sauce:

1½ (1-ounce) squares
  unsweetened chocolate
½ cup sugar
2 tablespoons hot water (105°
  to 115°)
½ cup hot milk (105° to 115°)
2 eggs, separated
Pinch of salt
1 teaspoon vanilla
  extract
½ cup whipping cream

Melt chocolate in top of a double boiler over boiling water. Add sugar, hot water, and milk, stirring well.

Beat egg yolks until thick and lemon colored. Gradually stir one-fourth of chocolate mixture into yolks; add to remaining chocolate mixture, stirring constantly. Cook over boiling water 15 minutes or until thickened and bubbly. Stir in salt. Remove from heat. Cool completely. Stir in vanilla.

Beat egg whites (at room temperature) until stiff, but not dry. Gently fold beaten whites into chocolate mixture.

Beat whipping cream until soft peaks form. Fold whipped cream into chocolate mixture. Chill. Yield: 2½ cups.

DATE TAPIOCA PUDDING

⅓ cup instant tapioca
3 cups cold water
2 cups firmly packed brown sugar
1 cup chopped dates
½ cup chopped pecans
Whipped cream

Combine tapioca, water, sugar, and dates in a small Dutch oven; stir well. Let stand 5 minutes.

Bring mixture to a boil; reduce heat. Cook, stirring constantly, until slightly thickened. Remove from heat; chill 1 hour. Stir in pecans. Chill until serving time.

Spoon into serving dishes, and top with whipped cream. Yield: 6 to 8 servings.

Fairview School, Birmingham, Alabama, had a coed cooking class as early as 1930.

PISTACHIO TAPIOCA PUDDING

6 almond macaroons, crushed
¼ cup chopped pistachio nuts
2 tablespoons sherry
1 cup milk
2 tablespoons instant tapioca
1 tablespoon plus 2 teaspoons sugar
½ teaspoon almond extract
1 cup whipping cream, whipped

Place macaroon crumbs and nuts in a medium mixing bowl. Add sherry, and mix well; set aside to soak.

Scald milk in a medium saucepan; stir in tapioca. Cook over low heat 15 minutes, stirring constantly. Remove from heat, and stir in sugar and almond extract; set aside to cool.

Fold whipped cream into cooled tapioca mixture. Spoon into four 6-ounce custard cups; top with macaroon-nut mixture. Chill. Yield: 4 servings.

Tapioca is made of the roots of manioc or cassava plants that grow in semitropical places like South and Central America, the West Indies, and Africa. Natives of these regions pound the roots to make a flour which is a staple of their diet. They use it as North Americans use wheat flour in breads and cakes. Purified, as we buy it, tapioca is almost pure starch. Along with sago, it was widely used by early American cooks, although they had to finish cleaning it before using. It also played a role in sickroom cookery, often appearing in old cookbooks in a chapter entitled "Cooking for Invalids."

SPICED AND STEAMED

COTTAGE PUDDING WITH LEMON SAUCE

¼ cup butter or margarine, softened
¾ cup sugar
1 egg
1¼ cups all-purpose flour
1 tablespoon baking powder
½ teaspoon salt
1 cup milk
½ teaspoon vanilla extract
Lemon Sauce

Cream butter in a mixing bowl; gradually add sugar, beating well. Add egg; beat well.

Combine flour, baking powder, and salt; add to creamed mixture alternately with milk, beginning and ending with flour mixture. Mix well after each addition. Stir in vanilla.

Pour batter into a greased and floured 8-inch square pan. Bake at 350° for 40 minutes or until a wooden pick inserted in center comes out clean. Cool in pan 10 minutes; remove from pan, and let cool completely. Cut into 2- x 4-inch bars. Place each bar on an individual serving plate, and spoon Lemon Sauce over top. Yield: 8 servings.

Lemon Sauce:

½ cup sugar
2 tablespoons cornstarch
Dash of salt
1 cup water
½ cup lemon juice
1 tablespoon butter or margarine, softened

Combine sugar, cornstarch, and salt in a small saucepan; mix well. Gradually add water and lemon juice; stir until smooth. Cook over low heat, stirring constantly, 10 minutes or until thickened. Add butter; stir until butter melts. Cool slightly. Yield: 1¾ cups.

APPLE PUDDING

6 medium-size cooking apples, peeled, cored, and sliced
1 cup butter or margarine, softened
1½ cups sugar
5 eggs, separated
1 cup milk
5 slices white bread, cut into 1-inch cubes
2 teaspoons grated lemon rind
2 tablespoons lemon juice
¼ teaspoon ground nutmeg
2 tablespoons finely chopped almonds (optional)
¼ cup plus 1 tablespoon sugar
½ teaspoon vanilla extract

Place apples in a large Dutch oven with water to cover; bring to a boil. Reduce heat; cover and simmer until apples are tender. Drain. Mash apples until pulpy. Cool slightly. Add butter, 1½ cups sugar, egg yolks, milk, bread cubes, lemon rind, juice, and nutmeg in a large mixing bowl; stir well. Stir in almonds, if desired. Spoon mixture into a greased 2-quart casserole. Bake, uncovered, at 350° for 1 hour or until firm. Remove from oven, and set aside.

Beat egg whites (at room temperature) until foamy. Gradually add ¼ cup plus 1 tablespoon sugar, 1 tablespoon at a time; beat until stiff peaks form. Fold in vanilla. Spread meringue over top of pudding. Return to oven, and bake an additional 10 minutes or until meringue is lightly browned.

Spoon into individual serving bowls. Serve hot or cold. Yield: 8 servings.

GINGER-APPLE PUDDING

½ cup butter or margarine
½ cup firmly packed brown sugar
2 eggs
1 cup molasses
2½ cups all-purpose flour
1½ teaspoons baking soda
½ teaspoon salt
1 (2.7-ounce) bottle crystallized ginger, finely chopped
1 cup boiling water
3 medium-size cooking apples, peeled, cored, and cut into eighths
2 tablespoons sugar, divided
2 tablespoons butter or margarine, divided
Vanilla ice cream

Cream butter in a large mixing bowl; gradually add brown sugar, beating until light and fluffy. Add eggs, one at a time, beating well after each addition. Add molasses; beat well.

Combine flour, soda, salt, and ginger; stir well. Add to creamed mixture alternately with boiling water, beginning and ending with flour mixture. (Batter will be thin.) Pour half of batter into a greased 13- x 9- x 2-inch baking dish; arrange half of apples over batter. Sprinkle with 1 tablespoon sugar, and dot with 1 tablespoon butter. Repeat procedure with remaining batter, apples, sugar, and butter.

Bake at 350° for 45 minutes or until a wooden pick inserted in center comes out clean. Cut into 3-inch squares. Transfer to serving plates; serve warm with ice cream. Yield: 12 servings.

Add these two apple puddings to your repertoire: Custardy Apple Pudding with a brown meringue (front) and Ginger-Apple Pudding. The crystallized ginger measurement is definitely correct; try it!

GINGER PUDDING

1 cup molasses
½ cup sugar
½ cup shortening
2 eggs
2½ cups all-purpose flour
1 teaspoon baking soda
1 teaspoon ground cloves
2 teaspoons ground
  cinnamon
2 teaspoons ground ginger
½ teaspoon salt
1 cup hot water
Lemon sauce or Hard Sauce
  (pages 136-37)

Combine molasses, sugar, shortening, and eggs in a large bowl; beat at high speed of an electric mixer until blended. Combine flour, soda, spices, and salt in a small bowl; stir well. Add flour mixture to creamed mixture alternately with hot water, beginning and ending with flour mixture; stir after each addition.

Pour pudding batter into a lightly greased 12- x 8- x 2-inch baking dish. Bake at 350° for 40 minutes or until a wooden pick inserted in center comes out clean. Cool slightly; cut into 4- x 3-inch bars. Serve with lemon sauce or Hard Sauce. Yield: 8 servings.

BISHOP WHIPPLE PUDDING

2 eggs, beaten
½ cup sugar
⅛ teaspoon salt
⅔ cup all-purpose flour
1 teaspoon baking powder
1 cup chopped dates
1 cup finely chopped pecans
1 teaspoon vanilla extract
Brown Sugar Sauce
Whipped cream or ice cream

Combine eggs, sugar, and salt in a medium mixing bowl; beat well. Combine flour, baking powder, dates, pecans, and vanilla; stir well. Gradually add flour mixture to egg mixture, stirring well. Spoon into a greased and floured 9-inch square pan. Bake at 350° for 30 minutes or until a wooden pick inserted in center comes out clean. Cool in pan 10 minutes. Remove from pan, and cool completely on a wire rack.

Cut pudding into 2¼-inch squares. Slice each square in half horizontally. Spoon 2 tablespoons Brown Sugar Sauce over the bottom half of each square. Replace top half of each square. Transfer to a serving plate, and serve with a dollop of whipped cream or a scoop of ice cream. Yield: 8 servings.

Brown Sugar Sauce:

¼ cup plus 2 tablespoons
  butter or margarine,
1½ cups firmly packed dark
  brown sugar
Pinch of salt
1 tablespoon hot water
¼ cup evaporated milk
1 teaspoon vanilla extract

Combine butter, sugar, and salt in a small saucepan. Cook over low heat 8 minutes or until sugar dissolves, stirring constantly. Stir in hot water. Remove from heat; cool slightly. Gradually add milk and vanilla; stir well. Yield: about 2 cups.

In the midst of dessert, this distinguished gathering pauses to pose for the photographer.

Date Pudding with Cherry Sauce is as rich as it is colorful, especially with a dollop of whipped cream.

DATE PUDDING WITH CHERRY SAUCE

1 cup chopped dates
1 cup boiling water
1 teaspoon baking soda
1 cup sugar
1 cup chopped pecans
1 egg, slightly beaten
3 tablespoons shortening, melted
¾ cup all-purpose flour
1 teaspoon vanilla extract
Cherry Sauce
Whipped cream

Combine dates, water, and soda in a small bowl; set aside. Combine sugar, pecans, egg, and shortening in a medium mixing bowl; stir until well blended. Add flour alternately with date mixture to sugar mixture, beginning and ending with flour. Stir in vanilla.

Pour mixture into a greased 9-inch square baking pan. Bake at 375° for 30 minutes or until a knife inserted in center comes out clean. Cool pudding in pan on a wire rack 10 minutes. Cut into 3-inch squares, and transfer to individual serving plates. Top with Cherry Sauce, and garnish with a dollop of whipped cream. Yield: 9 servings.

Cherry Sauce:

1 tablespoon butter or margarine, softened
1 cup sugar
1 (16-ounce) can pitted tart cherries, undrained
3 tablespoons cornstarch

Cream butter in a small saucepan; gradually add sugar, beating well. Drain cherries, reserving juice. Combine cherry juice and cornstarch, stirring until smooth. Add cherry juice mixture and cherries to sugar mixture; bring to a boil. Reduce heat; simmer, stirring frequently, until mixture thickens. Yield: about 2 cups.

WOODFORD PUDDING

3 eggs
1 cup sugar, divided
½ cup butter or margarine, softened
1 cup plum jam
½ cup all-purpose flour
1 teaspoon ground cinnamon
1 teaspoon ground nutmeg
Dash of ground cloves
1 teaspoon baking soda
3 tablespoons milk
Sweetened whipped cream or Hard Sauce (page 137)

Beat eggs in a medium mixing bowl 5 minutes or until very light and fluffy. Gradually add ½ cup sugar, beating well.

Cream butter in a large mixing bowl; gradually add remaining sugar, beating until light and fluffy. Add egg mixture and jam, beating well. Stir in flour, cinnamon, nutmeg, and cloves.

Dissolve soda in milk; add to batter, stirring well. Pour batter into a greased 2-quart casserole. Bake at 350° for 40 minutes or until set. (Pudding will rise, then fall.) Cut into squares; transfer to a serving plate, and serve warm with sweetened whipped cream or Hard Sauce. Yield: 6 to 8 servings.

SWEET POTATO PONE

2 eggs, beaten
½ cup firmly packed dark brown sugar
¼ cup butter or margarine, melted
2 cups grated raw sweet potatoes
1 cup milk
¼ teaspoon salt
½ teaspoon ground cinnamon
¼ teaspoon ground nutmeg
½ teaspoon vanilla extract
Whipped cream (optional)

Combine eggs, sugar, and butter in a mixing bowl, beating well; stir in next 6 ingredients.

Pour mixture into a well-greased 1-quart casserole. Bake, uncovered, at 325° for 45 minutes or until top is browned; stir top crust under. Bake an additional 50 minutes or until a knife inserted in center comes out clean. Spoon into serving bowls. Serve hot or cold with whipped cream, if desired. Yield: 4 to 6 servings.

PERSIMMON PUDDING

1¼ cups buttermilk
1 teaspoon baking soda
2 eggs, beaten
2 cups persimmon pulp
1½ cups all-purpose flour
1 teaspoon baking powder
1 teaspoon ground cinnamon
⅛ teaspoon salt
¼ cup whipping cream
2 cups sugar
¼ cup butter or margarine, melted
1 teaspoon vanilla extract
1 cup chopped walnuts
Creamy Vanilla Sauce

Combine buttermilk and soda in a small mixing bowl; stir well, and set aside.

Combine eggs and persimmon pulp in a large mixing bowl; stir well. Sift together flour, baking powder, cinnamon, and salt in a medium mixing bowl. Add dry ingredients to egg mixture alternately with buttermilk mixture, beginning and ending with flour mixture. Stir well after each addition. Stir whipping cream, sugar, butter, vanilla, and walnuts into batter; beat well.

Pour batter into a well-greased 2½-quart shallow baking dish. Bake at 350° for 45 minutes or until a knife inserted in center comes out clean. Cool in dish 10 minutes. Cut into 2½-inch squares, and transfer to a serving plate. Serve with Creamy Vanilla Sauce. Yield: 16 servings.

Creamy Vanilla Sauce:

¼ cup butter or margarine, softened
½ cup sifted powdered sugar
1 cup whipping cream
⅛ teaspoon vanilla extract

Cream butter in top of a double boiler. Add sugar, and beat well. Stir in whipping cream. Place over boiling water, and cook, beating constantly, until slightly thickened. Remove from heat, and stir in vanilla. Serve hot. Yield: 1⅓ cups.

Sunset Home Economics Club, Opelousas, Louisiana, made 57 yam dishes for 1948 "Yambilee."

Caramel Sponge Pudding made with caramelized sugar (front) vies with Lemon Sponge Pudding (rear) for top honors.

CARAMEL SPONGE PUDDING

1 cup sugar
¼ cup butter or margarine, softened
1 cup warm whipping cream (105° to 115°)
4 eggs, separated
¼ cup all-purpose flour
Pinch of salt
Whipped cream (optional)

Sprinkle sugar evenly into a 10-inch cast-iron skillet; place over medium heat. Cook, stirring constantly, with a wooden spoon until sugar melts and turns golden brown. Gradually add butter and whipping cream, stirring constantly, until mixture is well blended. Remove from heat, and set aside to cool.

Beat egg yolks in a large mixing bowl until thick. Gradually pour cooled caramelized mixture into yolks, adding alternately with flour and salt. Beat well after each addition.

Beat egg whites (at room temperature) and salt until stiff peaks form. Gently fold into caramelized mixture.

Pour mixture into a lightly greased 1-quart casserole. Place casserole in an 8-inch square baking pan, and fill with boiling water to a depth of 1 inch. Bake at 375° for 45 minutes. Spoon pudding into individual serving bowls, and garnish with a dollop of whipped cream, if desired. Serve hot or cold. Yield: 4 to 6 servings.

LEMON SPONGE PUDDING

1½ cups sugar
¼ cup plus 1½ teaspoons all-purpose flour
1½ cups milk
1 tablespoon plus 1½ teaspoons grated lemon rind
¼ cup plus 1½ teaspoons lemon juice
¾ teaspoon salt
3 eggs, separated

Combine sugar, flour, milk, lemon rind, juice, salt, and egg yolks in a large mixing bowl; beat well. Set aside.

Beat egg whites (at room temperature) until stiff peaks form. Gently fold beaten egg whites into reserved lemon mixture. Pour batter into an 8-inch square baking dish. Place baking dish in a pan of boiling water to come halfway up sides of dish. Bake, uncovered, at 325° for 40 minutes or until pudding is lightly browned; cool. Spoon pudding into individual serving bowls. Yield: 8 servings.

CHOCOLATE SPONGE PUDDING

3 tablespoons butter or
    margarine
½ (1-ounce) square
    unsweetened chocolate
1 cup sugar, divided
1 teaspoon vanilla extract
¾ cup all-purpose flour
1 teaspoon baking powder
½ teaspoon salt, divided
½ cup chopped pecans
¼ cup plus 2 tablespoons
    milk
½ cup firmly packed brown
    sugar
¼ cup plus 2 tablespoons
    cocoa
1¼ cups boiling water
Whipped cream (optional)

Melt butter and chocolate in top of a double boiler over boiling water, stirring constantly. Remove from heat; add ½ cup sugar and vanilla. Mix well; set aside.

Combine flour, baking powder, ¼ teaspoon salt, pecans, and milk in a medium bowl; stir well. Add chocolate; stir well. Pour into a greased 8-inch square pan.

Combine remaining sugar, salt, brown sugar, and cocoa; sprinkle over batter. Pour boiling water over topping; do not stir. Bake at 350° for 1 hour. Cool slightly; spoon into individual serving dishes. Top with whipped cream, if desired. Yield: 6 servings.

Grown in Central America, cacao pods contain cocoa beans.

STEAMED CHOCOLATE PUDDING

½ cup butter, softened
¾ cup sugar
¾ cup all-purpose flour
3 tablespoons cocoa
Dash of salt
3 eggs
½ teaspoon vanilla extract
¼ cup half-and-half
Brandy Sauce

Cream butter in a large mixing bowl; gradually add sugar, beating 5 minutes at medium speed of an electric mixer. Sift together flour, cocoa, and salt; add to creamed mixture alternately with eggs, beginning and ending with flour mixture. Beat well after each addition. Add vanilla and ¼ cup half-and-half, beating well.

Spoon mixture into a well-greased and floured 1½-quart pudding mold, and cover tightly with lid.

Place mold on rack in a large stockpot; add boiling water to a level even with bottom of rack. Bring to a boil. Cover; reduce heat to low; and simmer 2 hours, adding water as needed. Remove mold from water; let cool 2 minutes. Unmold onto a serving platter. Slice and serve with Brandy Sauce. Yield: 8 servings.

Brandy Sauce:

½ cup butter or margarine,
    softened
1 cup sugar
4 egg yolks
1 cup whipping cream
Pinch of salt
¼ cup brandy

Cream butter in top of a double boiler; gradually add sugar, beating well. Add egg yolks, one at a time, beating well after each addition. Add whipping cream and salt, beating well. Place over boiling water; cook, stirring constantly, until smooth and thickened. Remove from heat, and stir in brandy. Serve warm with Steamed Chocolate Pudding. Yield: 2¼ cups.

The John Dugosh family making molasses at the molasses mill, Bandera, Texas, c.1910.

CRANBERRY-MOLASSES PUDDING

¼ cup butter or margarine,
   softened
½ cup firmly packed brown
   sugar
½ cup molasses
1 egg
½ teaspoon baking soda
½ cup hot water
1½ cups all-purpose flour,
   divided
1 teaspoon baking powder
1 cup fresh cranberries,
   chopped
Rum Sauce

Cream butter in a large bowl. Add sugar and molasses; beat well. Add egg; beat well. Dissolve soda in water; add to creamed mixture, beating well.

Combine 1 cup flour and baking powder; stir into pudding mixture. Combine cranberries and remaining flour; toss lightly. Stir into batter. Pour batter into a well-greased 1½-quart steam pudding mold, and cover tightly with lid.

Place mold on a rack in a large stockpot with enough boiling water to come halfway up sides of mold. Cover stockpot. Place on bottom oven rack. Steam in oven at 350° for 3 hours. Remove mold from water; cool slightly. Remove lid from mold to allow steam to escape. Loosen pudding from sides of mold. Unmold onto a serving dish. Serve warm with Rum Sauce. Yield: 6 to 8 servings.

Rum Sauce:

½ cup butter or margarine
1 cup sugar
½ cup whipping cream
2 tablespoons rum

Melt butter in top of a double boiler over boiling water. Stir in sugar and cream; cook over boiling water, stirring frequently, 30 minutes or until thickened. Cool slightly; stir in rum. Serve warm. Yield: 1½ cups.

Molasses is a by-product of sugar manufacturing, ranging in flavor and color from light to dark as the processing continues. "First strike" is delicate in flavor; "second strike," favored by many Southern bakers, is stronger and darker. Sugarcane was grown in the Southern colonies, but sugar refinement first took place in Europe. In 1840, Norberto Rilleux of New Orleans developed the vacuum evaporation system, and sugar refinement began in this country. The centrifuge was added in the 1880s, and sugar became more affordable. Most Southerners hung onto their molasses jugs; times were still hard.

PLUM PUDDING

1 (16-ounce) package dark
  brown sugar
1 cup fine dry breadcrumbs
1 teaspoon baking soda
½ teaspoon salt
½ teaspoon ground allspice
½ teaspoon ground cinnamon
½ teaspoon ground nutmeg
½ teaspoon ground cloves
1 (10-ounce) package currants
1 cup raisins
1 cup golden raisins
2 (2-ounce) packages slivered
  almonds
1 cup all-purpose flour
½ pound beef suet, ground
1 cup milk
1 egg, beaten
Plum Pudding Sauce
Hard Sauce (page 137)

Combine brown sugar, breadcrumbs, soda, salt, and spices
in a large mixing bowl; stir well.
Set aside.

Dredge currants, raisins, and
almonds in flour, stirring to
coat well. Add to sugar mixture,
mixing well. Add beef suet,
milk, and egg, stirring until well
blended.

Pour mixture evenly into 2
greased 1-pound coffee cans.
Cover top of each can with a
damp cotton towel, and tie securely with string. Place cans on
a rack in a large stockpot; add
water to come halfway up sides
of cans. Cover stockpot; bring
water to a boil. Reduce heat to
medium; cover and simmer 3
hours.

Remove cans from stockpot;
remove towels to allow steam to
escape. Cool slightly. Loosen
pudding from sides of each can,
and invert onto a serving platter. Slice and serve with Plum
Pudding Sauce or Hard Sauce.
Yield: 16 to 20 servings.

Plum Pudding Sauce:

½ cup sugar
1 tablespoon all-purpose flour
½ cup water
Pinch of salt
1½ teaspoons butter or
  margarine, softened
1 tablespoon brandy

Combine sugar, flour, water,
and salt in a small saucepan.
Cook over medium heat, stirring constantly, until thickened. Remove from heat, and
stir in butter and brandy until
well blended. Serve hot. Yield:
about 1 cup.

STEAMED ENGLISH
PLUM PUDDING

1 cup milk, scalded
12 cups soft breadcrumbs
4 eggs
2 cups sugar
1 cup grape jelly
½ pound beef suet, finely
  chopped
Grated rind and juice of 1
  lemon
1¼ cups raisins
1 (10-ounce) package currants
2 (4-ounce) packages chopped
  candied citron
1 (4-ounce) package chopped
  candied orange peel
1¾ cups all-purpose flour,
  divided
1 teaspoon baking soda
1 cup hot coffee
1 teaspoon salt
1 teaspoon ground cinnamon
1 teaspoon ground nutmeg
Sauce (recipe follows)

Combine milk and bread-
crumbs in a large mixing bowl;
set aside. Combine eggs and
sugar in a small mixing bowl;
beat at medium speed of an electric mixer until well blended.
Add egg mixture, jelly, beef suet,
and lemon rind and juice to
breadcrumb mixture, stirring
until well combined.

Dredge raisins, currants, citron, and orange peel in ¾ cup
flour; set aside. Dissolve soda in
coffee. Combine remaining
flour, salt, and spices; add to
breadcrumb mixture alternately
with coffee mixture, beginning
and ending with flour mixture.
Stir in dredged fruit mixture.

Spoon batter evenly into 4
greased 1-pound coffee cans.
Cover top of each can with a
damp cotton towel, and tie securely with string. Place cans on
a rack in a large stockpot; add
boiling water to come halfway
up sides of cans. Cover and
steam in oven at 350° for 4
hours.

Remove cans from stockpot;
remove towels to allow steam to
escape. Cool slightly. Loosen
pudding from sides of each can,
and invert onto a serving platter. Slice and serve with sauce.
Yield: four 1-pound steamed
puddings.

Sauce:

½ cup butter or margarine,
  softened
1 cup sugar
1 egg yolk
½ teaspoon vanilla extract
¼ cup boiling water
1 cup whipping cream,
  whipped

Cream butter in top of a double boiler; gradually add sugar,
beating well. Add yolk and vanilla, beating until well blended.
Stir in water. Place over boiling
water; cook, stirring occasionally, until smooth. Remove from
heat, and cool to room temperature. Chill.

Immediately before serving,
fold in whipped cream. Yield:
about 6 cups.

Christmas Pudding, ready to be served warm with Wine Sauce.

CHRISTMAS PUDDING

½ cup butter or margarine,
  softened
1 cup sugar
4 eggs
2¼ cups all-purpose flour,
  divided
1 teaspoon baking soda
¼ teaspoon ground allspice
¼ teaspoon ground cinnamon
¼ teaspoon ground cloves
½ cup commercial sour
  cream
1½ cups raisins, chopped
Wine Sauce

Cream butter in a large mixing bowl; gradually add sugar, beating well. Add eggs, one at a time, beating well after each addition.

Combine 1¾ cups flour, soda, and spices; add to creamed mixture alternately with sour cream, beginning and ending with flour mixture. Dredge raisins in remaining flour, and fold into batter. Spoon batter into a well-greased 1½-quart steamed pudding mold, and cover tightly with lid.

Place mold on rack in a large stockpot with enough boiling water to come halfway up sides of mold. Cover stockpot; bring water to a boil. Reduce heat, and let simmer 3 hours. Remove mold from water, and cool slightly. Loosen pudding from sides of mold. Unmold onto a serving plate. Slice pudding and serve warm with Wine Sauce. Yield: 10 servings.

Wine Sauce:

1 egg
½ cup sugar
1 tablespoon water
½ cup butter or margarine
¼ cup Burgundy or other
  dry red wine

Combine egg, sugar, and water in top of a double boiler; beat well. Add butter; cook over boiling water, stirring frequently, 30 minutes or until sauce thickens. Remove from heat; stir in wine. Serve warm. Yield: 1¼ cups.

D eeply ingrained in the Southern heritage is English plum pudding, the most wonderfully misnamed dessert of all. There are no plums in it, of course, though there were plums available. Plums meant raisins or currants, by popular usage. It also meant cleaning and stoning them! Some old recipes specify Zante currants, those imported from the island of Zante, off the Greek coast.

FLAVOR OF FRUIT

It could be said that fruit has meant dessert since Eden's halcyon days. More to the point, fresh raw fruit has been reserved for last from Roman days through today, no matter how many courses were offered, or how many "made" sweet dishes were eaten along with those courses. Fresh fruit, nuts, and wine were placed on the polished wood tables after the cloths were taken away in the well-ordered mansions of the antebellum South.

Most of the exquisite fruit knives, some with ivory handles, so useful in the Old South dessert service, are seen now only in antique shops. But we find still that fresh fruit in season fits our "do something quick for dessert" life-style. Ambrosia, our classic Spanish-American dessert, is still divinely refreshing after all these years.

But what sweet ways we have of cooking those fruits, be they fresh, canned, or frozen! Hannah Glasse, in *The Art of Cookery*, 1747, sieved and sweetened stewed gooseberries and then mixed them with cream to make a "fool." Other berries work as well. Our folks got off the boat knowing about dumplings to drop into stewing fruit. North and South have colloquial names, origins unclear, for some old favorites. Northerners bake a "slump" of crust-topped fruit and turn it out upside-down for serving. They also stew blueberries with dumplings dropped in, to make a "grunt," which Southerners would likely call blueberry dumplings.

As for the mysterious "pandowdy," it is said to have begun as a deep-dish pie which, half-baked, was removed from the oven, the top broken up (dowdied), and baked off. In Mrs. Porter's *New Southern Cookery Book*, 1871, a Virginia author reached above Mason and Dixon's line and borrowed the pandowdy, giving a recipe for a "governor," the top crust of which is broken up and stirred into the filling.

Apple dumplings and berry roly-polies were boiled long before they were baked. Brown Betty, a modest spin-off from the ancient apple charlotte, remains a fine thing to do with leftover bread.

With fruit for dessert, you can't blame your sweet tooth for acting up.

Of all our flowering plants, the fragrant Magnolia grandiflora *is most symbolic of the South. And of our fruits, the citrus family. Add berries, melons, peaches . . . succulent Southerners all.*

FRESH AND CHILLED

AMBROSIA

12 large seedless oranges,
   peeled and sectioned
1 coconut, cracked, peeled,
   and grated
½ cup sugar

Combine all ingredients in a large serving bowl; mix well. Cover and refrigerate overnight.

Spoon mixture into stemmed dessert glasses. Serve chilled. Yield: 8 servings.

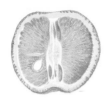

HOLIDAY AMBROSIA

1 (8-ounce) can pineapple
   chunks, undrained
1 coconut, cracked, peeled,
   grated, and divided
4 large seedless oranges,
   peeled and sectioned
2 bananas, sliced
½ cup sugar

Drain pineapple, reserving juice; set aside juice and chunks. Reserve ¼ cup grated coconut.

Arrange half of orange sections in bottom of a glass 1½-quart serving bowl. Top with half of pineapple chunks, coconut, bananas, and sugar. Repeat layers with remaining ingredients, pouring reserved pineapple juice over top and sprinkling with reserved coconut. Cover and refrigerate overnight. Spoon fruit mixture into individual serving bowls, and serve chilled. Yield: 6 servings.

*Sunrise Compote
combines fresh flavors
of fruit and sherbet,
the perfect dessert
for a summer luncheon.*

SUNRISE COMPOTE

3 ruby grapefruits, peeled,
   seeded, and sectioned
2 large oranges, peeled,
   seeded, and sectioned
1 large banana, sliced
1 (8-ounce) can pineapple
   slices, undrained and
   quartered
2 limes
½ cup apple juice
Raspberry or lime sherbet

Combine grapefruit, oranges, banana, and pineapple with juice in a large bowl. Cut 1 lime in half; cut one half into thin slices, and add to fruit mixture. Juice remaining limes, and add juice to fruit mixture. Discard rind and pulp. Stir in apple juice. Cover and refrigerate at least 2 hours.

Spoon fruit mixture into 8 stemmed dessert glasses. Top each with a scoop of desired sherbet. Serve immediately. Yield: 8 servings.

Fruit in Green Compote,
*an appliquéd quilt
detail from a Baltimore
album quilt, c.1903.*

AMBROSIAL ORANGES

6 medium oranges
½ cup slivered almonds,
  toasted
½ cup flaked coconut
½ cup chopped dates
½ cup Grand Marnier

Cut a thin slice from the bottom of each orange so orange will sit upright. Cut a 1-inch slice from tops of oranges. Gently remove orange pulp, leaving shells intact. Remove seeds; chop pulp.

Combine pulp, almonds, coconut, dates, and Grand Marnier; mix well. Spoon mixture into orange cups; chill thoroughly. Yield: 6 servings.

Naturalist John Bartram noted in 1765 that the wild Florida orange was a "relishing morsel," not knowing, apparently, that seeds had come from Spain on the earliest voyages of Hernando de Soto and Ponce de Leon. Spanish law decreed later that ships coming to the New World should carry seedlings, as the seeds dried out too much to be depended upon. Orange desserts have been in use in the South since before the Revolutionary War. When coconuts, early imports, met oranges, ambrosia was the result.

APRICOT FOOL

3 cups peeled and mashed
   apricots
¼ cup Triple Sec or other
   orange-flavored liqueur
1 cup whipping cream
2 tablespoons sugar
Grated rind of 1 lemon
½ (1-ounce) square semisweet
   chocolate

Combine apricots and liqueur in a large mixing bowl; stir well.

Beat 1 cup whipping cream in a small mixing bowl until foamy; gradually add sugar, beating until soft peaks form. Fold sweetened whipped cream and lemon rind into apricot mixture.

Spoon apricot mixture into 6 stemmed dessert glasses. Lightly grate chocolate over top of each serving. Chill thoroughly. Yield: 6 servings.

CANTALOUPE MELON CUPS

½ cup commercial sour
   cream
2 tablespoons honey
½ teaspoon grated orange
   rind
1 tablespoon orange juice
1 teaspoon lemon juice
¼ teaspoon dry mustard
Dash of salt
3 cantaloupes, cut into halves
   and seeded, leaving a 1-inch
   shell
1 pint whole strawberries,
   hulled and sliced
2 bananas, sliced
1 cup fresh blueberries

Combine sour cream, honey, orange rind and juice, lemon juice, mustard, and salt in a small mixing bowl, stirring well. Cover and chill mixture at least 1 hour.

Cut away a small slice from bottom of each cantaloupe half so melon cups will sit upright. Arrange sliced strawberries, bananas, and blueberries in each melon cup. Chill. Pour honey sauce over fruit before serving. Yield: 6 servings.

Fresh Peaches with Raspberries: The ultimate combination.

WATERMELON BOWL

1 (16-ounce) can dark, sweet
   cherries, undrained
1 tablespoon rum
1 large watermelon half
1 cantaloupe, halved, peeled,
   seeded, and cut into
   wedges
1 honeydew, halved, seeded,
   and scooped into balls
1 pint whole strawberries,
   washed and hulled
1 ripe papaya, peeled, seeded,
   and sliced
1 ripe pear, peeled, seeded,
   and sliced

Drain cherries, reserving juice in a small mixing bowl. Set cherries aside. Add rum to cherry juice; mix well. Set aside.

Cut a small slice from bottom of watermelon half so bowl will sit upright. Remove seeds and watermelon pulp from rind, leaving "watermelon bowl" intact. Cut watermelon pulp into large cubes; set aside.

Using a sharp paring knife, cut a scallop design around edge of watermelon bowl. Arrange watermelon cubes, cherries, cantaloupe wedges, honeydew balls, strawberries, sliced papaya, and pear slices in watermelon bowl. Pour cherry juice mixture evenly over fruit. Chill thoroughly. Serve fruit from watermelon bowl using a slotted spoon. Yield: 15 to 20 servings.

FRESH PEACHES WITH RASPBERRIES

3 large, ripe unpeeled
    peaches
1 pint fresh raspberries
Sifted powdered sugar
Nasturtium leaves (optional)

Wipe outer skin of each peach; slice each in half. Remove pit and discard.

Place each peach half on a serving plate or in a compote. Roll raspberries in powdered sugar, and arrange in center of each peach half. Garnish with nasturtium leaves, if desired. Serve chilled. Yield: 6 servings.

*Fresh fruit abounds
in this colorful
Mexican market scene.*

The strawberry is not native only to America. Some believe it simply spread throughout the Northern Hemisphere. Virginia strawberries (*Fragaria virginiana*) grew more thickly here than in Europe. An Englishman complained, "Wee can not sett downe foote but tred on strawberries." Cultivation of this strawberry began around 1600. Hybridization started in the 1700s in France. The hybrid strawberry we eat today has been bred to withstand shipping.

ROSE HILL STRAWBERRIES

1 (8-ounce) carton
    commercial sour
    cream
¼ cup maple syrup
3 pints whole strawberries,
    washed and hulled
2½ tablespoons firmly
    packed brown sugar

Combine sour cream and ¼ cup maple syrup in a small mixing bowl, mixing until well blended. Cover and refrigerate at least 1 hour.

Arrange strawberries in 8 dessert bowls. Sprinkle brown sugar evenly over strawberries; chill. Pour sour cream mixture over strawberries before serving. Yield: 8 servings.

First rule for strawberry pickers: Wear a hat. Wickliffe, Kentucky, c.1903.

FROSTED STRAWBERRIES

2 quarts whole strawberries
1¼ cups sugar, divided
½ cup cold water
2 egg whites
¼ teaspoon baking powder
½ teaspoon lemon extract

Wash strawberries, leaving stems intact. Drain. Pat dry with paper towels; set aside.

Combine 1 cup sugar and water in a heavy saucepan. Cook over medium heat, stirring frequently, until mixture comes to a boil and sugar dissolves. Continue cooking until mixture reaches thread stage (234°). Remove from heat, and set aside.

Beat egg whites (at room temperature) in top of a double boiler until stiff peaks form. Gradually add remaining sugar, beating well after each addition. While beating at medium speed of electric mixer, slowly pour hot syrup in a thin stream over egg whites. Beat until well blended. Fold in baking powder.

Place frosting over boiling water; beat constantly at high speed of an electric mixer 5 minutes or until stiff peaks form. Remove frosting from heat, and stir in lemon extract.

Dip strawberries in frosting; place on waxed paper to dry. (Do not refrigerate.) Place strawberries in individual dessert dishes, and serve immediately. Yield: about 16 servings.

STRAWBERRIES IN WINE

1½ quarts fresh strawberries, washed, hulled, and halved
1 cup sifted powdered sugar
1 cup Concord or other sweet red wine
1 teaspoon grated lemon rind
1 cup whipping cream
2 tablespoons sugar

Place strawberry halves in a large bowl; sprinkle with powdered sugar. Combine wine and lemon rind; pour over strawberries. Cover and refrigerate at least 1 hour.

Beat whipping cream until foamy; gradually add 2 tablespoons sugar, beating until soft peaks form.

Spoon strawberry mixture equally into 8 stemmed dessert glasses. Top with sweetened whipped cream. Serve immediately. Yield: 8 servings.

STRAWBERRIES À LA MODE

1 quart whole strawberries
1 tablespoon sugar
2 tablespoons brandy
2 tablespoons Triple Sec or other orange-flavored liqueur
¼ cup vanilla ice cream, slightly softened
¼ cup raspberry sherbet, slightly softened
1 cup whipping cream, whipped

Place strawberries in a large colander; submerge colander in cold water several times until berries are free of any excess debris. Drain berries. Reserve 6 pretty berries. Hull and coarsely slice remaining berries.

Place sliced strawberries in a shallow 2-quart bowl. Combine sugar, brandy, and Triple Sec; pour over berries. Cover bowl tightly, and refrigerate at least 3 hours.

Combine vanilla ice cream and raspberry sherbet; stir into berry mixture. Spoon into individual serving bowls. Dollop each serving with whipped cream, and garnish with reserved whole strawberries. Yield: 6 servings.

ALLEN'S
STRAWBERRY
CATALOGUE
SPRING
1903

KANSAS

A June scene at Allen's plant farms. Hoeing strawberries.

EXCELSIOR.—The best of all early berries. Eleven acres picked in 1902 55,902 qts., an average of 5,082 qts. per acre.

W.F. ALLEN
SALISBURY,
MARYLAND.

COOKING WITH FRUIT

STUFFED BAKED APPLES

6 medium-size cooking
  apples, peeled and cored
¼ cup plus 2 tablespoons
  prepared mincemeat,
  divided
¼ cup plus 2 tablespoons
  sugar, divided
1 cup boiling water
Lemon Hard Sauce

Place apples in a 9-inch
square baking pan. Stuff each
apple with 1 tablespoon mincemeat. Sprinkle each apple with
1 tablespoon sugar. Pour boiling water in bottom of pan.
Bake at 350° for 45 minutes or
until apples are tender. Place
apples in individual serving
bowls, and serve hot with
Lemon Hard Sauce. Yield: 6
servings.

Lemon Hard Sauce:

¼ cup butter or margarine,
  softened
1 cup sifted powdered sugar
⅛ teaspoon salt
1 teaspoon milk
1 teaspoon lemon extract

Cream butter in a medium
mixing bowl. Add sugar and
salt; beat well. Gradually add
milk, and beat until creamy.
Stir in lemon extract. Chill.
Yield: ½ cup.

APPLE CRISP

5 cups peeled, cored, diced
  cooking apples
1 teaspoon ground
  cinnamon
½ cup water
1 cup all-purpose flour
1 cup sugar
½ cup butter or margarine
Vanilla ice cream or shredded
  Cheddar cheese (optional)

Place apples in a lightly
greased 8-inch square baking
pan; sprinkle apples with cinnamon. Pour water over apples.
Combine flour and sugar; cut
in butter with a pastry blender
until mixture resembles coarse
meal. Sprinkle over apple mixture. Bake at 350° for 1 hour.
Spoon into individual serving
bowls, and serve hot with ice
cream or cheese, if desired.
Yield: 6 servings.

APPLE CRUMBLE

4 medium-size cooking
  apples, peeled, cored, and
  thinly sliced
¾ cup all-purpose flour
1 cup sugar
1 teaspoon baking
  powder
¾ teaspoon salt
1 egg, beaten
⅓ cup butter or margarine,
  melted
Ground cinnamon
Whipping cream (optional)

Place apples in a greased 2-
quart casserole; set aside.
Sift together flour, sugar,
baking powder, and salt in a
small mixing bowl. Stir in egg to
form a crumb mixture; sprinkle
crumb mixture evenly over
apples. Pour melted butter over
top, and sprinkle with ground
cinnamon.
Bake at 350° for 35 minutes.
Spoon into individual serving
bowls, and serve hot with whipping cream, if desired. Yield: 6
to 8 servings.

Young worker takes his pick of the apple crop, c.1900.

*A showy apple
crate label proclaims
the virtues of the
Queen Shenandoah brand.*

CLASSIC APPLE CHARLOTTE

14 slices bread, lightly
   toasted
½ cup butter or margarine,
   melted and divided
8 medium-size cooking
   apples, peeled, cored, and
   thinly sliced
¾ cup sugar
1 tablespoon lemon juice
1 cup applesauce
1 teaspoon ground cinnamon
Sweetened whipped cream

Trim and discard crust from bread. Cut each slice of bread in half lengthwise. Brush both sides of bread slices with ¼ cup melted butter, and arrange half of slices over bottom and sides of a 2-quart charlotte mold. Set remaining buttered bread slices aside.

Combine remaining melted butter and apples in a large skillet; cook over medium heat 10 minutes, stirring frequently. Sprinkle sugar and lemon juice over apples. Cook over medium heat, stirring frequently, until apples are tender and sugar has turned to syrup.

Spoon half of apple mixture into prepared charlotte mold. Combine applesauce and cinnamon; spoon over first apple layer. Spoon remaining apple mixture over applesauce mixture, and top with reserved buttered bread slices. Cover with aluminum foil. Bake at 400° for 10 minutes. Reduce heat to 375°, and bake an additional 30 minutes. Remove from oven; uncover and let cool completely in mold on a wire rack. Invert onto a serving platter, and top with whipped cream. Yield: 8 to 10 servings.

APPLE PANDOWDY

4 cups peeled, cored, and
  thinly sliced cooking apples
2 cups sugar
1 teaspoon ground cinnamon
½ cup water
2 cups all-purpose flour
1 tablespoon plus 1 teaspoon
  baking powder
¾ teaspoon salt
¼ cup plus 2 tablespoons
  shortening
¾ cup milk
Additional sugar
1 tablespoon butter or
  margarine

Arrange apples evenly in a
lightly greased 10- x 6- x 2-inch
baking dish. Combine 2 cups
sugar and cinnamon; sprinkle
over apples. Pour water over
apples, and set aside.

Combine flour, baking powder, and salt; stir well. Cut in
shortening with a pastry
blender until mixture resembles
coarse meal. Sprinkle milk
evenly over flour mixture, stirring until dry ingredients are
moistened.

Turn dough out onto a floured
surface; knead 8 to 10 times.
Roll dough to a 10- x 6-inch rectangle, and place on top of
apples. Cut slits in dough to
allow steam to escape. Sprinkle
with additional sugar, and dot
with butter.

Bake at 300° for 1 hour; remove from oven. Preheat broil-
ing unit. Broil top crust 6 to 7
inches from heating element 3
minutes or until lightly
browned. Spoon into individual
serving bowls, and serve immediately. Yield: 8 servings.

*An apple grower in
Hambersham County,
Georgia, put on this apple
picking demonstration, 1923.*

APPLE BROWN BETTY

5 cups peeled, cored, and
  sliced cooking apples
5 cups soft breadcrumbs,
  divided
1¾ cups sugar
1 teaspoon ground cinnamon
½ cup butter or margarine,
  divided
½ cup water, divided
Whipping cream

Arrange half of apples in a
lightly greased 12- x 8- x 2-inch
baking dish. Sprinkle with half
of breadcrumbs. Combine sugar
and cinnamon; sprinkle half of
sugar mixture over bread-
crumbs. Dot with half of butter,
and sprinkle with half of water.
Repeat layers.

Bake at 400° for 45 minutes
or until apples are tender.
Spoon into individual serving
bowls, and serve warm with
whipping cream. Yield: 8 to 10
servings.

Apple Pandowdy opens up to reveal warm, spicy sliced fruit.

OZARK PUDDING

1 egg, beaten
¾ cup sugar
⅓ cup all-purpose flour
1¼ teaspoons baking
   powder
⅛ teaspoon salt
½ cup grated unpeeled apple
½ cup raisins
½ cup chopped pecans
1 teaspoon vanilla extract
Sweetened whipped cream

Combine egg and sugar in a medium mixing bowl. Beat until light and fluffy. Sift together flour, baking powder, and salt; add to egg mixture, and beat well. Stir in apple, raisins, pecans, and vanilla.

Pour batter into a well-greased 1-quart casserole. Bake at 350° for 30 minutes. Spoon into individual serving dishes, and top with whipped cream. Yield: 4 to 6 servings.

Pecans are for sale at this roadside market, 1929, Willingham Fruit Farm, Peach County, Georgia.

HUGUENOT TORTE

2 eggs
1 cup sugar
¼ cup all-purpose flour
2 teaspoons cream of tartar
1½ teaspoons baking soda
¼ teaspoon salt
1 teaspoon lemon juice
1 teaspoon vanilla extract
1 cup chopped apple
1 cup chopped pecans
Whipped cream
Additional chopped pecans

Beat eggs in a large mixing bowl at high speed of electric mixer for 8 minutes. Gradually add sugar, beating well. Combine flour, cream of tartar, soda, and salt in a small mixing bowl; stir well. Gradually add flour mixture to egg mixture, beating until smooth. Stir in lemon juice, vanilla, apple, and 1 cup pecans.

Pour batter into a lightly greased 13- x 9- x 2-inch baking pan. Bake at 325° for 35 minutes. (Torte will rise, then fall.) Remove from oven, and cool completely. Cut into 3-inch squares. Transfer to individual serving plates; serve with a dollop of whipped cream and additional chopped pecans. Yield: about 12 servings.

The Huguenots, the protestants of France, were infused by Lutheran ideas. In 1685, after more than 100 years of warring with the French Catholic Church, the Huguenots were forced into exile. Of those who came to America, the majority settled in the Carolinas. Charleston is a unique culinary island; the food is a mix of French recipes and the talent of the black cooks who refined them. Huguenot Torte is one of the regional foods we celebrate in these pages.

PECAN NUTS
WILLINGHAM FRUIT FARM

Baked Bananas with Lemon Sauce: What a delicious surprise!

BAKED BANANAS WITH LEMON SAUCE

½ cup sugar
2 teaspoons ground
   cinnamon
6 small firm bananas, peeled
Pastry (recipe follows)
1 egg white, slightly beaten
Lemon Sauce
Zest of 1 lemon
Fresh mint leaves (optional)

Combine sugar and cinnamon; roll bananas in sugar mixture to coat well. Set aside.

Roll pastry out on a heavily floured surface to ⅛-inch thickness; cut pastry into six equal portions. Gently wrap a portion around each coated banana. Moisten edges with water; pinch gently to seal.

Place bananas, seam side down, on a well-greased 15- x 10- x 1-inch jellyroll pan. Brush liberally with egg white. Bake at 475° for 8 minutes or until lightly browned.

Transfer bananas to a serving platter. Top with Lemon Sauce; sprinkle with lemon zest. Garnish with mint leaves, if desired. Yield: 6 servings.

Pastry:

2 cups all-purpose flour
½ teaspoon salt
½ teaspoon sugar
¾ cup butter
¼ cup plus 2 tablespoons
   shortening
¼ cup ice water

Sift together dry ingredients in a medium mixing bowl. Cut in butter and shortening with a pastry blender until mixture resembles coarse meal. Sprinkle with ice water, and stir just until dry ingredients are moistened. Shape pastry into a ball. Chill at least ½ hour. Yield: pastry for 6 bananas.

Lemon Sauce:

¾ cup sugar
1½ tablespoons cornstarch
½ cup water
2 egg yolks
1½ tablespoons butter or
   margarine, softened
¼ cup lemon juice

Combine sugar and cornstarch in a medium-size heavy saucepan; mix well. Add water; bring to a boil. Reduce heat; cook, stirring constantly, until slightly thickened.

Beat yolks until thick and lemon colored. Gradually stir one-fourth of hot mixture into yolks; add to remaining hot mixture. Continue cooking over medium heat, stirring constantly, until sauce thickens.

Remove from heat. Add butter and lemon juice; stir until well blended. Chill until ready to use. Yield: about 1 cup.

BANANAS IN WINE

3 very firm bananas, peeled
   and cut in half lengthwise
2 tablespoons butter or
   margarine
2 tablespoons firmly packed
   brown sugar
⅛ teaspoon ground cinnamon
¼ cup white wine
Sweetened whipped cream

Sauté banana halves in butter in a large skillet until golden brown and tender. Sprinkle with sugar and cinnamon. Add wine, and simmer until sauce thickens. Serve bananas warm with whipped cream. Yield: 4 servings.

Celebrate the blueberry season with a dish of Blueberry Grunt and squares of Blueberry Buckle.

BLUEBERRY PUDDING

¼ cup butter or margarine
1 cup sugar
2 eggs, beaten
½ cup commercial sour
  cream
2 cups all-purpose flour,
  divided
½ teaspoon baking
  soda
½ teaspoon cream
  of tartar
2 cups fresh blueberries
Hard Sauce (page 137)

Cream butter; gradually add sugar, beating well. Add eggs; beat well. Stir in sour cream.

Combine 1 cup flour, soda, and cream of tartar; stir well. Add flour mixture to creamed mixture; beat well.

Combine blueberries and remaining flour; toss until blueberries are well coated. Fold blueberries into batter. Spoon into a well-greased 1½-quart ovenproof mold.

Bake, uncovered, at 350° for 1 hour and 10 minutes or until a wooden pick inserted in center comes out clean. Cool in mold 10 minutes; remove from pan, and cool completely. Transfer pudding to a serving dish; slice and serve warm with Hard Sauce. Yield: 8 servings.

BLUEBERRY GRUNT

¼ cup plus 2 tablespoons
  butter or margarine
1 cup all-purpose flour
1 cup sugar
2 teaspoons baking powder
⅛ teaspoon salt
¾ cup milk
4 cups fresh blueberries
Sweetened whipped cream

Preheat oven to 375°. Place butter in an 8-inch square baking dish; place dish in oven just until butter melts. Remove from oven, and cool 10 minutes.

Combine flour, sugar, baking powder, and salt in a large mixing bowl; add milk, and mix well. Pour batter into prepared baking dish; sprinkle blueberries over batter. Bake at 375° for 30 minutes or until golden brown. Spoon dessert into individual serving dishes; serve warm with whipped cream. Yield: 8 servings.

BLUEBERRY BUCKLE

¼ cup shortening
1¾ cups sugar, divided
1 egg
½ cup milk
2⅔ cups all-purpose flour,
  divided
2 teaspoons baking powder
½ teaspoon salt
2 cups fresh blueberries
1 teaspoon ground cinnamon
½ cup butter or margarine

Cream shortening in a medium mixing bowl; add ¾ cup sugar and egg, beating well. Add milk, and beat well. Combine 2 cups flour, baking powder, and salt; add to creamed mixture, mixing well. Fold in blueberries. Spread mixture into a greased and floured 13- x 9- x 2-inch baking pan.

Combine remaining sugar, flour, and cinnamon in a small mixing bowl. Cut in butter with a pastry blender until mixture resembles coarse meal. Sprinkle over blueberry mixture in pan. Bake at 375° for 45 minutes. Cool. Cut into squares to serve. Yield: 12 to 15 servings.

The blueberry, indigenous to America, came as a grand surprise to the English. The shrubby bush comes in many species, with shiny or downy leaves that turn to blazes of color in the fall. In some parts of the country, the name is used interchangeably with huckleberry, though properly the latter is a smaller berry of another genus with hard, crackly seeds. The Indians dried them for winter; the settlers found many uses for them.

CRANBERRY COMPOTE

3 cups water
1½ to 2 cups sugar
2 medium-size cooking
   apples, peeled, cored, and
   cubed
2 oranges, peeled, sliced, and
   seeded
2 cups fresh cranberries

Combine water and sugar in a large saucepan. Bring to a boil. Reduce heat, and cook 5 minutes. Add apples, and cook 5 minutes. Add oranges and cranberries; cook an additional 10 minutes. Remove from heat. Let cool, and refrigerate until thoroughly chilled. Spoon into individual serving bowls. Yield: 8 servings.

FRESH GUAVA COBBLER

1½ cups sugar, divided
2 cups peeled, sliced guava
   (about 5 small)
⅓ cup butter or margarine
¾ cup all-purpose flour
2 teaspoons baking powder
½ teaspoon salt
¾ cup milk
Whipping cream

Combine ½ cup sugar and sliced guava in a small mixing bowl; toss lightly to coat well. Set aside.

Preheat oven to 350°. Place butter in a 2-quart casserole; place in oven until butter melts. Remove from oven, and set aside.

Combine remaining sugar, flour, baking powder, and salt in a small mixing bowl; add milk, and stir just until dry ingredients are moistened.

Carefully pour batter over melted butter in casserole. Spoon sugared guava evenly over top of batter. Bake at 350° for 1 hour. (Batter will rise up over fruit, and become crisp brown.) Spoon into individual serving dishes, and serve with whipping cream. Serve immediately. Yield: 6 servings.

MANGO FLAMEADOR

1 tablespoon butter or
margarine
1 tablespoon sugar
½ orange
½ lime
2 tablespoons Cointreau or
Triple Sec
1 large mango, peeled and
cubed
2 tablespoons tequila
Coconut ice cream

Melt butter in a large skillet or chafing dish; add sugar, and cook over medium heat until bubbly.

Peel and juice orange and lime halves; reserve peel and juice. Add peel to skillet. Stir in Triple Sec; ignite with a long match. When flames die down, add juice of orange and lime. Cook over medium heat until thickened and lightly browned. Remove fruit peels; discard. Add mango; bring to a boil.

Place tequila in a small, long-handled pan; heat just until warm. Ignite with a long match, and pour over mango mixture. Baste mango with sauce until flames die down. Serve immediately over coconut ice cream. Yield: 2 servings.

BAKED PEACHES

4 cups peeled, sliced fresh
peaches
1 tablespoon butter or
margarine
1 cup firmly packed brown
sugar
¼ cup water
¼ cup Chablis or other dry
white wine
Grated rind and juice of 1
lemon
½ teaspoon ground mace
Sweetened whipped cream

Place peaches in a 1½-quart casserole; dot with butter. Combine sugar, water, wine, lemon rind and juice, and mace; mix well. Pour over peaches.

Bake, uncovered, at 350° for 30 minutes or until peaches are tender. Spoon into individual serving dishes using a slotted spoon. Dollop with sweetened whipped cream. Yield: 4 to 6 servings.

PEACH CRISP

6 cups peeled, sliced fresh
peaches
1 cup sifted all-purpose flour
1 cup sugar
½ teaspoon ground cinnamon
¼ teaspoon salt
½ cup butter or margarine,
softened
Whipping cream

Place peaches in a lightly-greased 8-inch square baking dish; set aside.

Combine flour, sugar, cinnamon, and salt in a medium mixing bowl; cut in butter with a pastry blender until mixture resembles coarse meal. Sprinkle mixture evenly over peaches in prepared dish. Bake at 375° for 45 minutes or until golden brown. Spoon into individual serving bowls; serve warm with whipping cream. Yield: 6 to 8 servings.

*Mango Flameador for
a taste of the tropics.
A glamorous flambé on
coconut ice cream.*

Fruit, Bird and Dwarf Pear Tree *by Charles V. Bond, 1856.*

PEACH TART

Pastry for one 9-inch pie
1 egg, separated
1½ pounds fresh peaches, peeled and sliced
1 tablespoon lemon juice
¼ cup sugar
¼ cup firmly packed brown sugar
1 teaspoon ground cinnamon
Pinch of ground nutmeg
Pinch of ground cloves
Pinch of salt
2 tablespoons butter or margarine
¼ cup whipping cream, warmed

Roll dough to ⅛-inch thickness on a lightly floured surface. Fit pastry into a 9-inch tart pan or pieplate.

Brush inside of shell with unbeaten egg white. Arrange peaches in shell; sprinkle with lemon juice.

Combine sugar, cinnamon, nutmeg, cloves, and salt; sprinkle over peaches. Dot with butter. Bake at 350° for 25 minutes.

Combine whipping cream and egg yolk, beating well with a wire whisk. Pour mixture over peaches. Continue baking at 350° for 20 minutes or until set. Cool to room temperature. Cut into wedges to serve. Yield: one 9-inch tart.

Mrs. Porter's *New Southern Cookery Book,* 1871, "borrowed" the Northern pandowdy and called it a governor: "Peach Governor . . . Line a deep dish with rich thick crust; pare and cut into halves or quarters some juicy, rather tart peaches; put in sugar, spices and flavoring to taste; stew it slightly, and put it in the lined dish. . . . " She put on a crust, baked it, and then gave instructions to "break up the top crust into small pieces and stir it into the fruit; serve hot or cold." She suggested sauces from cream to brandy to assorted fruit sauces.

PEAR CRUMBLE

1½ cups gingersnap cookie
   crumbs
¼ cup butter or margarine,
   melted
2 cups sugar
4 cups water
¼ teaspoon salt
6 medium pears, peeled,
   cored, and cubed
1 tablespoon lemon juice
½ cup firmly packed brown
   sugar
½ teaspoon ground
   cinnamon
¼ teaspoon ground nutmeg
Vanilla ice cream

Combine cookie crumbs and butter in a small mixing bowl; mix well. Press half of mixture into bottom of a lightly greased 8-inch square baking dish; reserve remaining mixture, and set aside.

Combine 2 cups sugar, water, and salt in a medium saucepan; cook until sugar dissolves. Add pears; cook over medium heat 15 minutes or just until pears are tender.

Remove saucepan from heat, and drain, reserving ¼ cup syrup. Place pears in prepared dish; pour lemon juice and reserved syrup over top. Combine brown sugar, cinnamon, and nutmeg; sprinkle over pears. Top with remaining cookie crumb mixture.

Bake at 350° for 25 minutes. Spoon into individual serving dishes, and serve warm with ice cream. Yield: 6 to 8 servings.

Poached Pears are as simple to make as they are delicious.

POACHED PEARS

4 ripe pears
2 tablespoons lemon juice
1 large lemon, thinly sliced
2 cups water
2 cups sugar
2 (4-inch) sticks cinnamon
16 whole allspice

Peel pears, removing core from bottom end but leaving stem intact. Slice ¼ inch from bottom of each pear to make a flat base. Brush pears with lemon juice to prevent browning; set pears aside.

Combine remaining ingredients in a large saucepan; bring to a boil. Add pears and cook, uncovered, over medium heat 20 minutes or until tender.

Remove pears to a warm serving dish using a slotted spoon. Continue cooking liquid over medium heat 15 minutes or until slightly thickened. Remove whole spices from syrup mixture, and discard. Pour syrup mixture over pears. Yield: 4 servings.

RHUBARB CRUMBLE

3 cups sliced rhubarb
¼ teaspoon ground cinnamon
¾ cup sugar
¾ cup all-purpose flour
¼ cup plus 2 tablespoons
  butter or margarine
Vanilla ice cream

Arrange rhubarb evenly in bottom of a greased 1-quart casserole; sprinkle with cinnamon. Set aside.

Combine sugar and flour; cut in butter until mixture resembles coarse meal. Sprinkle sugar mixture evenly over rhubarb. Bake at 450° for 15 minutes. Reduce temperature to 375°, and bake an additional 25 minutes or until lightly browned. Spoon into serving bowls while warm, and top with ice cream. Yield: 4 servings.

PRUNE WHIP

1 cup dried pitted prunes
4 egg whites
¼ teaspoon salt
½ cup sifted powdered sugar
1 teaspoon vanilla extract
2 tablespoons chopped
  pecans
Sweetened whipped cream

Combine prunes and water to cover in a heavy saucepan. Bring to a boil. Reduce heat; cover and simmer 30 minutes. Drain and cool.

Place prunes in container of an electric blender, and process until smooth. Set aside.

Beat egg whites (at room temperature) and salt until foamy; gradually add sugar, beating until soft peaks form.

Stir vanilla into prune puree; gently fold beaten egg whites into prune mixture. Spoon mixture into a 1½-quart casserole. Bake at 325° for 15 minutes or until puffed and set. Cool to room temperature, and chill. Spoon into individual serving dishes. Sprinkle with pecans, and top with whipped cream. Yield: 6 servings.

BRANDIED NECTARINES

10 medium nectarines
1 cup sugar
1 cup water
½ cup plus 2 tablespoons
  brandy, divided
2 tablespoons vanilla extract
½ cup whipping cream
2 tablespoons sifted
  powdered sugar
Fresh raspberries
Mint leaves

Place nectarines in a wire basket or cheesecloth, and dip into boiling water 1 minute. Plunge nectarines in cold water; drain. Remove skin.

Combine nectarines, sugar, and water in a medium saucepan; bring to a boil. Reduce heat, and simmer 1 minute. Stir in ½ cup brandy and vanilla; chill thoroughly.

Drain nectarines, and place each in a chilled individual dessert dish. Combine whipping cream, powdered sugar, and remaining brandy, mixing well. Spoon over nectarines. Garnish with raspberries and mint leaves. Yield: 10 servings.

An Early American painted tinware tray, c.1830.

CLASSIC CUSTARDS & SOUFFLÉS

Custard takes many forms, each more delicious than the other. Next to ambrosia, boiled custard may be the most typically "Southern" of all desserts. Actually, it is not boiled at all, but is stirred over gentle heat to keep the egg thickener from lumping. Boiled or "stirred" custard is not only good as an end in itself, served with a spot of grated nutmeg, it is also a basic ingredient in our traditional trifles and in many of our ice cream recipes.

There are many old recipes that combine custard with cooked fruit. Fruit is usually used to make a bottom layer, a custard mixture is poured over it, and, when baked almost done, a meringue is laid on and browned. Another slant on the custard-with-fruit idea is the time-honored Bird's Nest Pudding, which appeared in Mrs. Porter's *New Southern Cookery Book* in 1871. Whole cored apples are placed in the "pudding basin," the custard is poured around them, and the whole baked together.

Baked custard is cooked at low heat, the mold standing in hot, not boiling, water. For generations before ovenproof glass bakeware was invented, housewives baked their individual "cup" custards in regular teacups.

Some of our classic Southern desserts make it impossible for us to deny our English beginnings: Trifles and their varied "tipsy" offshoots, Floating Island, the cup custards — coconut was a favored additive — even the chocolate custard are rooted in Hannah Glasse's English best-seller of 1747, *The Art of Cookery.*

Other major delights in this chapter point up the influence of the French: Soufflés, Crème Brûlée, and that wondrous confection, Caramel Custard, baked in a mold lined with caramelized sugar and turned upside-down for serving, or, as the French term *crème renversée* implies, reversed. The Spanish invented it, too, and called it flan.

Strictly Spanish as well is the glorious Fried Custard, *crema frita*. Another version, *leche frita* or fried milk, is thickened with cornstarch, not eggs. Which is the ultimate temptation? Avoid guesswork; try them all.

Custards go from simply delectable, as in Boiled Custard (in cup), to extravagant heights: At left, a Grand Floating Island, crowned with a gossamer of spun sugar, and a Classic English Trifle (right) are sheer grandeur.

CUSTARDS, BOILED AND BAKED

BOILED CUSTARD

½ cup sugar
2 tablespoons all-purpose
  flour
6 eggs, beaten
3 cups milk
1 teaspoon vanilla extract
Ground nutmeg

Combine sugar and flour in a medium-size heavy saucepan; stir well. Add eggs and milk; stir with a wire whisk until all ingredients are blended.

Cook over medium-low heat, stirring constantly with a metal spoon, 15 minutes or until mixture begins to thicken and coats the spoon.

Remove from heat immediately, and stir in vanilla. Cool to room temperature. Chill. Pour custard into chilled cups, and sprinkle with nutmeg. Yield: about 6 cups.

SOFT BOILED CUSTARD

3 cups milk
1 cup whipping cream
4 eggs
1 cup sugar
1 teaspoon vanilla extract
Ground nutmeg

Combine milk and whipping cream in top of a double boiler. Cook over boiling water, stirring constantly, until milk mixture is warm. Combine eggs and sugar in a small mixing bowl; beat well.

Gradually stir one-fourth of hot milk mixture into egg mixture; add to remaining hot milk mixture, stirring well. Cook over boiling water, stirring constantly with a metal spoon, until mixture begins to thicken and coats the spoon. Remove from heat, and stir in vanilla. Cool to room temperature; chill.

Pour custard into chilled cups, and sprinkle with nutmeg. Yield: about 6 cups.

Custard is ready when it coats a metal spoon.

VANILLA CUSTARD

3 eggs, beaten
¾ cup sugar
1 tablespoon all-purpose flour
2 cups milk
1 cup whipping cream
1 teaspoon vanilla extract
2 tablespoons slivered
  almonds, toasted (optional)

Combine eggs and sugar in top of a double boiler; beat well. Add flour, stirring until smooth.

Gradually stir in milk and whipping cream. Cook over boiling water, stirring constantly with a metal spoon, 10 minutes or until mixture thickens and coats the spoon. Remove from heat; stir in vanilla.

Pour mixture into six 6-ounce custard cups. Cover and chill thoroughly. Before serving, sprinkle with almonds, if desired. Yield: 6 servings.

EASY BOILED CUSTARD

4 cups milk, divided
⅓ cup cornstarch
1 (14-ounce) can
  sweetened condensed
  milk
3 eggs, separated
1 teaspoon vanilla
  extract
Dash of salt

Combine 1 cup milk and cornstarch in top of a double boiler, stirring until well blended. Add remaining 3 cups milk and sweetened condensed milk; stir well. Cook over boiling water, stirring constantly, until mixture thickens and is smooth.

Beat egg yolks slightly. Gradually stir one-fourth of hot milk mixture into yolks; add to remaining hot milk mixture, stirring constantly. Cook over boiling water, stirring constantly with a metal spoon, until mixture thickens and coats the spoon. Remove from heat, and stir in vanilla and salt. Set custard aside and let cool to room temperature.

Beat egg whites (at room temperature) until until stiff peaks form. Gently fold egg whites into cooled custard mixture; chill thoroughly. Spoon custard into individual serving bowls to serve. Yield: 10 to 12 servings.

Inventor Gail Borden, the man behind the milk, was a notable American. Born in New York in 1801, he came to Texas to help survey the land for Austin, and he laid out the city of Galveston. Back in New York in 1851, he began his work with milk. In 1856, he patented canned evaporated milk and the following year opened for business in Connecticut as Gail Borden, Jr. & Co. His product was invaluable to the Union Army in the Civil War; its uses spread later, proving to be a godsend to islanders off the East Coast, the Florida Keys, and in other remote places where cows did not thrive. Borden's familiar Eagle Brand Milk was the ingredient that made the original Florida key lime pie possible.

Borden, Inc.

Collection of Business Americana

BUTTERSCOTCH CUSTARD

¾ cup firmly packed brown
  sugar
3 tablespoons all-purpose
  flour
1 egg, beaten
1¾ cups milk
¼ cup butter or margarine,
  softened
1 teaspoon vanilla extract
Chopped peanuts (optional)

Combine sugar, flour, and egg in top of a double boiler; add milk. Cook over boiling water, stirring constantly, until thickened and smooth. Remove from heat; add butter and vanilla. Stir until butter melts.

Spoon butterscotch mixture into individual dessert cups, and serve warm or chilled. Sprinkle with chopped peanuts, if desired. Yield: 4 servings.

CREAMY CHOCOLATE CUSTARD

1 cup sugar
2 tablespoons all-purpose
  flour
Pinch of salt
2 cups milk
2 (1-ounce) squares
  semisweet chocolate,
  melted
6 egg yolks
1 teaspoon vanilla extract
Grated white chocolate
  (optional)

Combine sugar, flour, and salt in a medium saucepan. Add milk, and cook over medium heat, stirring constantly, until candy thermometer registers 170°. Remove mixture from heat, and stir in melted chocolate. Cool.

Place egg yolks in top of a double boiler, and beat slightly. Slowly add chocolate mixture to beaten egg yolks, stirring constantly. Cook over boiling water, stirring constantly, until mixture thickens and is smooth. Remove from heat, and stir in vanilla.

Spoon mixture into four individual dessert bowls. Cool to room temperature. Cover and chill thoroughly. Sprinkle with grated chocolate, if desired. Yield: 4 servings.

Creamy Chocolate Custard (foreground) is garnished with grated white chocolate while Butterscotch Custard takes to a peanut topping.

KISS PUDDING

4 eggs, separated
3 tablespoons cornstarch
4 cups milk
2 tablespoons butter or
    margarine, softened
½ cup sugar

Combine egg yolks and cornstarch in a large heavy saucepan; beat well. Gradually add milk, stirring constantly. Cook over medium heat, stirring constantly with a metal spoon, 2 minutes or until mixture thickens and coats the spoon. Remove from heat; add butter, and stir until butter melts. Pour mixture into an 8-inch square baking dish.

Beat egg whites (at room temperature) until foamy. Gradually add sugar, 1 tablespoon at a time, until stiff peaks form. Spread meringue over hot pudding. Bake at 350° for 10 minutes or until lightly browned. Cool to room temperature. Spoon into individual serving bowls. Yield: 8 to 10 servings.

A Southerner will not have to search his memory too strenuously to remember a childhood fraught with creamy banana pudding and egg kisses, crisp cookies made of the same sugar-egg white combination we use for meringue glacé. From meringue as kisses to meringue-topped pudding was but a short leap: Suddenly there was Kiss Pudding. Soft and sweet it is.

BIRD'S NEST PUDDING

8 medium-size cooking
    apples, unpeeled and cored
1 cup plus 2 tablespoons
    sugar, divided
3½ tablespoons cornstarch
4 cups milk
1 egg, separated
3 eggs, beaten
1½ teaspoons sugar

Place apples in a 12- x 8- x 2-inch baking dish; fill centers of cored apples evenly using ½ cup sugar. Pour water into baking dish to a depth of ½ inch. Bake at 350° for 45 minutes. Remove from oven; drain off syrup, and discard. Drain baked apples of any excess moisture; return to baking dish. Set aside.

Combine ½ cup plus 2 tablespoons sugar and cornstarch in top of a double boiler; stir well. Add milk, mixing well. Set 1 egg white aside in a small mixing bowl. Add egg yolk and beaten eggs to milk mixture; beat well using a wire whisk.

Place over boiling water and cook, stirring constantly with a metal spoon, 20 minutes or until mixture thickens and coats the spoon.

Pour custard evenly around apples in baking dish. Beat reserved egg white (at room temperature) until foamy. Gradually add 1½ teaspoons sugar, beating until soft peaks form. Dollop meringue on top of each apple.

Bake at 350° for 8 minutes or until meringue is lightly browned. Remove from oven, and spoon a baked apple and custard into individual serving bowls. Serve immediately. Yield: 8 servings.

53

Bonnie Slotnick

BANANA CUSTARD PUDDING

2½ cups sugar
½ cup all-purpose flour
¼ cup cornstarch
7 cups milk
4 egg yolks, lightly beaten
¼ cup butter or margarine, softened
1 teaspoon vanilla extract
1 (12-ounce) package vanilla wafers
9 medium bananas, peeled and sliced

Combine sugar, flour, and cornstarch in a medium mixing bowl. Mix well, and set aside.

Pour milk into a large Dutch oven; cook over medium heat until candy thermometer registers 160°. Gradually stir one-fourth of hot milk into yolks; stir into reserved dry ingredients, and add to remaining hot milk. Cook, stirring constantly, until mixture thickens and coats the spoon. Remove from heat, and stir in butter and vanilla. Let cool to room temperature.

Line bottom of a 13- x 9- x 2-inch baking dish with one-third of wafers. Arrange half of banana slices over wafers; top with half of cooled custard. Repeat layers, reserving remaining one-third of wafers to crumble and sprinkle over custard. Chill thoroughly. Spoon into individual serving bowls. Yield: 20 to 25 servings.

Inside a Dothan, Alabama, grocery store in 1912, the fresh fruits are the richest feature. Tropical bananas hang upside down, opposite from the way they grew.

BANANA CREAM PUDDING

½ cup sugar
3 tablespoons cornstarch
3 cups milk
2 eggs, beaten
1 (12-ounce) package vanilla
  wafers
4 large bananas, peeled and
  sliced
1 cup whipping cream,
  whipped

Combine sugar and cornstarch in top of a double boiler; add milk and eggs, beating well with a wire whisk. Place over boiling water and cook, stirring constantly with a metal spoon, until mixture thickens and heavily coats the spoon. Remove from heat, and let cool to room temperature.

Line bottom of a 2-quart baking dish with one-third of vanilla wafers. Arrange half of sliced bananas over wafers; top with half each of custard and whipped cream. Repeat layers, reserving remaining one-third of vanilla wafers to garnish top of pudding.

Cover and refrigerate at least 5 hours. Spoon into individual serving bowls, and serve chilled. Yield: 10 servings.

Elegant desserts evolved slowly from the early puddings, waiting mostly for refined sugar. Even kings did not often have dessert tables, for up until about 1700, sugar was sold in concrete-like cones weighing 8 to 10 pounds and was so precious that it was kept locked up against theft. Needless to say, sugared goodies were the province of the moneyed class, the "upper crust." Meanwhile, those in tighter straits used molasses and sorghum.

Bonnie Slotnick

PEACH CUSTARD

1 (29-ounce) can peach
  halves, drained and chopped
4 eggs, separated
1½ cups sugar, divided
3 tablespoons cornstarch
4 cups milk, scalded
½ teaspoon vanilla extract

Place peaches evenly in bottom of a lightly greased 2-quart casserole; set aside.

Combine egg yolks, 1 cup sugar, and cornstarch in a large heavy saucepan; beat well. Gradually add milk, stirring constantly. Cook over medium heat, stirring constantly with a metal spoon, 1 minute or until mixture begins to thicken and coat the spoon. Remove from heat, and cool slightly. Pour custard mixture over peaches; set aside.

Beat egg whites (at room temperature) until foamy. Gradually add remaining sugar, 1 tablespoon at a time, beating until stiff peaks form. Add vanilla; beat well. Spread meringue over custard, sealing to edge of casserole. Bake at 400° for 5 minutes or until meringue is lightly browned. Spoon into individual serving bowls, and serve immediately. Yield: 8 to 10 servings.

Bonnie Slotnick

ORANGE CUSTARD

5 oranges, peeled, seeded,
  and separated into sections
½ cup plus 2 tablespoons
  sugar, divided
1 cup milk
2 eggs, separated
1 tablespoon plus 1 teaspoon
  cornstarch

Place orange sections in a medium bowl; sprinkle with 2 tablespoons sugar. Set aside.

Combine milk, egg yolks, ¼ cup sugar, and cornstarch in a saucepan; mix well. Cook over medium heat, stirring constantly with a metal spoon, 5 minutes or until custard thickens and coats spoon. Cool to room temperature.

Drain prepared oranges; discard juice. Place oranges in bottom of a 1-quart casserole. Pour cooled custard over oranges. Set aside.

Beat egg whites (at room temperature) until foamy. Gradually add remaining sugar, 1 tablespoon at a time, beating until stiff peaks form. Spread meringue over top of custard, sealing to edges. Bake at 450° for 5 minutes or until golden brown. Spoon into individual serving bowls. Yield: 4 to 6 servings.

BAKED CUP CUSTARD

2 eggs, beaten
¼ cup sugar
¼ teaspoon salt
2 cups milk, scalded
½ teaspoon vanilla
   extract
Ground nutmeg

Combine eggs, sugar, and salt in a medium mixing bowl; beat with a wire whisk until well combined. Add milk and vanilla, beating until well blended.

Pour custard evenly into six 6-ounce custard cups. Sprinkle top of each custard with ground nutmeg. Place custard cups in a 13- x 9- x 2-inch baking pan. Add warm water to pan to a depth of 1 inch.

Bake at 325° for 1 hour or until a knife inserted between center and edge of custard comes out clean. Remove cups from water; serve hot or chilled. Yield: 6 servings.

BAKED COCONUT CUP CUSTARD

¼ cup plus 2 tablespoons
   grated coconut, divided
2 eggs, lightly beaten
2 cups milk
½ cup sugar
¼ teaspoon vanilla
   extract
Sweetened whipped
   cream

Place 1 tablespoon coconut in bottom of six 6-ounce custard cups; set aside.

Combine eggs, milk, sugar, and vanilla in a medium mixing bowl; mix well. Pour into prepared custard cups, and place in a 13- x 9- x 2-inch baking pan. Pour hot water into pan to a depth of 1 inch. Bake at 325° for 1 hour and 30 minutes or until a knife inserted halfway between center and edge of custard comes out clean. Remove cups from water immediately; cool to room temperature. Chill thoroughly. Dollop with sweetened whipped cream before serving. Yield: 6 servings.

Photographer: Mary-Gray Hunter

Connemara Baked Custard forms its own brown sugar sauce.

CONNEMARA BAKED CUSTARD

4 eggs, beaten
½ cup sugar
2½ cups milk
1 teaspoon vanilla
   extract
½ teaspoon salt
2 tablespoons firmly packed
   light brown sugar
Ground nutmeg

Combine eggs and sugar, beating well. Gradually add milk, beating well. Stir in vanilla and salt.

Place 1 teaspoon brown sugar in bottom of six 6-ounce custard cups; pour custard evenly into custard cups. Sprinkle each custard with nutmeg.

Place custard cups in a 13- x 9- x 2-inch baking pan; pour cold water into pan to a depth of 1 inch. Bake at 300° for 1½ hours or until a knife inserted halfway between center and edge of custard comes out clean. Remove cups from water; cool to room temperature. Chill thoroughly. Turn custard out onto individual serving plates to serve. Yield: 6 servings.

C arl August Sandburg, born in 1878, lived by his own rules, this rugged wanderer, poet, salesman, biographer of Lincoln, winner of two Pulitzer prizes, and true American hero. Typically, one of his 38 definitions of poetry was " . . . the achievement of the synthesis of hyacinths and biscuits." In 1945, Sandburg and his wife, Paula, bought Connemara, an antebellum estate in Flat Rock, North Carolina, where they lived until his death in 1967. Our dessert, a family favorite, was often served at Connemara.

Carl Sandburg Home NHS, National Park Service

June Glenn, Jr.

MOCHA MACAROON CUSTARD

3 eggs, separated
1 egg yolk
½ cup sugar
1½ cups milk, scalded
½ cup strong coffee
1 teaspoon vanilla extract
¼ cup plus 1 tablespoon
    coconut macaroon crumbs
1½ tablespoons sugar
¼ cup whipping cream,
    whipped
¼ teaspoon vanilla extract
Additional macaroon crumbs

Set 1 egg white aside in a small mixing bowl.

Combine remaining egg whites and yolks in a medium mixing bowl. Add ½ cup sugar to egg mixture; beat until well blended. Stir in scalded milk, coffee, 1 teaspoon vanilla, and ¼ cup plus 1 tablespoon macaroon crumbs.

Pour mixture into a lightly greased 1-quart casserole. Place in an 8-inch square baking pan; add warm water to a depth of 1 inch. Bake at 300° for 1 hour and 10 minutes or until a knife inserted halfway between center and edge comes out clean. Remove casserole from water immediately; cool to room temperature. Chill thoroughly.

Beat reserved egg white (at room temperature) until foamy. Gradually add 1½ tablespoons sugar, beating until stiff peaks form. Fold in whipped cream and ¼ teaspoon vanilla. Spread over top of custard. Sprinkle additional macaroon crumbs over top. Spoon custard into individual serving bowls; serve immediately. Yield: 6 servings.

Trade card, c.1890.

Collection of Kit Barry

BAKED RAISIN CUSTARD

2 cups milk
2 eggs, beaten
¼ cup sugar
Pinch of salt
½ teaspoon vanilla extract
1 slice bread, cubed
½ cup raisins
Ground cinnamon
Ground nutmeg

Combine milk, eggs, sugar, salt, and vanilla in a medium mixing bowl; beat well with a wire whisk. Stir in bread cubes and raisins.

Pour mixture into a lightly greased 1-quart casserole. Sprinkle with cinnamon and nutmeg. Place in an 8-inch square baking pan. Add warm water to pan to a depth of 1 inch.

Bake at 350° for 1 hour or until a knife inserted halfway between center and edge comes out clean. Spoon into individual serving dishes, and serve immediately. Yield: 4 to 6 servings.

JUST FOR COMPANY

A HEN'S NEST

6 large eggs in the shell
Blancmange
Soft Custard
Candied orange peel

Carefully pierce small end of each egg shell using a long sharp needle. Continue to insert needle throughout entire length of egg, piercing yolk and opposite end of shell. Withdraw needle; carefully chip away hole at each end of shell to ⅛-inch circumference, using needle. Blow gently through one hole, forcing egg white and yolk to be expelled from hole at opposite end of shell. Reserve yolks and whites of 2 eggs for use in Soft Custard recipe. Other yolks and whites may be used in other recipes.

Rinse egg shells well; drain. Seal hole in small end of each shell using a small piece of freezer tape. Place egg shells, tape side down, in egg carton.

Pour blancmange equally into prepared egg shells. (Holes in shells may need to be enlarged.) Refrigerate overnight.

Pour a small amount of Soft Custard into 6 individual serving dishes. Sprinkle each with candied orange peel to resemble straw. Gently "unpeel" blancmange eggs, discarding shells. Arrange eggs over candied peel so that each serving resembles an egg in a hen's nest. Serve chilled. Yield: 6 servings.

Blancmange:

3 tablespoons sugar
2½ tablespoons cornstarch
⅛ teaspoon salt
1¼ cups milk
½ teaspoon vanilla extract

Combine sugar, cornstarch, and salt in a medium-size heavy saucepan. Gradually add milk. Cook over medium heat, stirring constantly, until mixture thickens. Cook an additional 2 to 3 minutes. Remove from heat, and stir in vanilla. Cool slightly. Yield: 6 servings.

Soft Custard:

2 eggs, beaten (reserved from blown egg shells)
1 cup milk
¼ cup sugar
⅛ teaspoon salt
1 teaspoon vanilla extract

Combine eggs, milk, sugar, and salt in top of a double boiler; beat until well blended, using a wire whisk. Place over boiling water and cook, stirring constantly with a metal spoon, until mixture thickens and coats the spoon. Remove from heat immediately, and stir in vanilla. Chill thoroughly. Yield: about 1¼ cups.

Spring flowers and a nest of eggs express Easter greetings, c.1900.

May yours be a joyful Easter

GRAND FLOATING ISLAND

3 eggs, separated
¼ teaspoon salt
2 cups sugar, divided
5 cups milk, divided
1 teaspoon vanilla extract

Beat egg whites (at room temperature) until soft peaks form; gradually add salt and ¼ cup sugar, 1 tablespoon at a time, beating until stiff peaks form. Set aside.

Heat 4 cups milk in a large saucepan to simmering. Drop egg white islands by tablespoonfuls into simmering milk. Cook each island 2 minutes on each side or until slightly firm. Remove islands with a slotted spoon, and drain on paper towels. Refrigerate until ready to serve.

Add remaining milk to hot milk in saucepan; heat to simmering. Combine egg yolks and ¾ cup sugar in a medium mixing bowl; beat until thick and lemon colored. Gradually stir one-fourth of hot milk into yolk mixture; add to remaining hot milk, stirring constantly. Cook, stirring constantly, over low heat 20 minutes or until thickened. Let mixture cool slightly, and stir in vanilla. Chill mixture thoroughly.

Sprinkle remaining 1 cup sugar evenly in a 10-inch cast-iron skillet; place over medium heat. Cook, stirring constantly with a wooden spoon, until sugar melts and turns light brown. Remove from heat.

Hold 2 dinner forks back to back. Dip the forks into the syrup, and as the syrup runs off, pull the forks apart, allowing the threads to spin down on a sheet of waxed paper. Repeat procedure until desired number of threads are spun. (If the syrup hardens, reheat to the syrupy stage over medium heat.)

Spoon chilled custard into a serving bowl. Mound islands on top of custard; top with spun sugar. Serve immediately. Yield: 8 servings.

TARBORO TIPSY CAKE

8 eggs, separated
Grated rind and juice of 1 lemon
1½ cups sugar
1½ cups all-purpose flour
1½ teaspoons baking powder
Pinch of salt
¾ cup milk
2 cups whole blanched almonds
1 cup plus 1 tablespoon sherry, divided
Boiled Custard
1 cup whipping cream
1 tablespoon powdered sugar
Whole maraschino cherries
Slivered almonds, toasted

Place egg yolks in a large mixing bowl; beat at high speed of an electric mixer 6 minutes or until thick and lemon colored. Add lemon rind and juice; beat at high speed an additional 4 minutes.

Gradually add sugar, 2 tablespoons at a time, beating 5 minutes or until smooth.

Combine flour, baking powder, and salt; add to yolk mixture alternately with milk, beginning and ending with flour mixture. Mix well after each addition.

Beat egg whites (at room temperature) until soft peaks form. Gently fold 1 cup of egg whites into yolk mixture. Gently fold yolk mixture into remaining egg whites.

Pour batter into an ungreased 10-inch tube pan, spreading batter evenly with a spatula. Bake at 375° for 50 minutes or until cake springs back when lightly touched. Remove cake from oven, and invert pan. Cool cake 40 minutes, and remove from pan.

Press almonds into sides and top of cake; place cake in a 12-cup trifle bowl. Immediately before serving, pour 1 cup sherry evenly over cake. Spoon Boiled Custard over cake and into hole in center of the cake.

Beat whipping cream until foamy; gradually add powdered sugar, beating until soft peaks form. Fold in remaining sherry.

Top cake with sweetened whipped cream, and garnish with maraschino cherries and toasted almonds. Spoon into serving bowls, and serve immediately. Yield: 12 to 15 servings.

Note: Slivered toasted almonds may be used in place of blanched almonds.

Boiled Custard:

8 egg yolks, beaten
1 cup sugar
¼ cup all-purpose flour
Pinch of salt
4 cups milk, scalded
1 teaspoon vanilla extract

Combine egg yolks, sugar, flour, and salt in top of a double boiler; stir until well blended. Slowly pour ¼ cup scalded milk into yolk mixture, stirring with a wire whisk until mixture is smooth. Slowly pour remaining scalded milk into yolk mixture, stirring constantly.

Place over boiling water and cook, stirring with a metal spoon, until mixture thickens and coats the spoon. Remove from heat, and stir in vanilla. Cool custard to room temperature, and chill thoroughly. Yield: about 4 cups.

Tarboro Tipsy Cake can be baked a day ahead and sauced with sherry and custard just before serving.

Nineteenth-century trade card.

TIPSY PARSON

2 eggs, beaten
½ cup sugar
1 tablespoon cornstarch
2½ cups milk
1 teaspoon vanilla extract
1 (3-ounce) package
  ladyfingers, split
  lengthwise
¼ cup sherry
Fresh strawberries

Combine eggs, sugar, and cornstarch in top of a double boiler, beating well. Gradually add milk, stirring constantly. Cook over boiling water, stirring constantly with a metal spoon, 20 minutes or until mixture coats the spoon. Cool slightly. Stir in vanilla. Cool completely.

Sprinkle 12 ladyfinger halves with sherry. Let stand 5 minutes. Line sides of a 1-quart soufflé dish with soaked ladyfingers; pour in custard. Top with remaining ladyfingers. Chill completely. Garnish with strawberries. Spoon into individual serving bowls. Yield: 6 servings.

CLASSIC ENGLISH TRIFLE

1 cup butter, softened
1½ cups sugar
5 eggs
1½ tablespoons lemon juice
½ teaspoon vanilla extract
¼ teaspoon almond extract
2 cups sifted cake flour
¼ teaspoon salt
¾ cup golden sherry, divided
3 cups fresh strawberries,
  washed, hulled, and halved
Boiled Custard
1 cup strawberry preserves
1½ cups whipping cream,
  whipped
Fresh whole strawberries,
  washed and drained

Cream butter in a medium mixing bowl; gradually add sugar, beating until light and fluffy. Add eggs, one at a time, beating well after each addition. Add lemon juice, vanilla, and almond extract, beating well.

Combine cake flour and salt; gradually add to creamed mixture, beating constantly. Beat at medium speed of an electric mixer 8 to 10 minutes. Pour batter into a greased 10-inch tube pan. Bake at 325° for 1 hour and 10 minutes or until cake tests done. Cool in pan 15 minutes. Remove from pan; cool completely on a wire rack.

Slice cake into ¼-inch slices; trim and discard crust. Line the bottom of a 16-cup trifle bowl with one-third of cake slices; sprinkle with ¼ cup sherry. Arrange strawberry halves, cut side out, around lower edge of bowl. Spoon 2 cups Boiled Custard over cake slices; place one-third of cake slices over custard. Gently spread strawberry preserves over cake; top with remaining cake slices. Pour remaining sherry over surface of trifle. Spoon remaining custard on top. Cover and chill.

Top trifle with whipped cream and garnish with whole strawberries. Serve immediately. Yield: 12 to 15 servings.

Boiled Custard:

2 cups milk
⅔ cup whipping cream
4 eggs
⅔ cup sugar
½ teaspoon vanilla extract

Combine milk and whipping cream in a medium saucepan. Cook over low heat until milk is warm. Combine eggs and sugar, beating well. Gradually stir one-fourth of warm milk mixture into eggs; add to remaining hot mixture, stirring constantly.

Cook over low heat, stirring constantly until mixture thickens and coats the spoon. Remove from heat; stir in vanilla. Cool to room temperature; chill. Yield: about 4 cups.

CRÈME BRÛLÉE

8 egg yolks
½ cup firmly packed dark brown sugar
¼ teaspoon salt
2 cups whipping cream, scalded
2 cups half-and-half, scalded
1 tablespoon vanilla extract
¾ cup firmly packed light brown sugar

Combine egg yolks, dark brown sugar, and salt in a large mixing bowl; beat well. Gradually add whipping cream and half-and-half, stirring constantly. Stir in vanilla.

Pour custard into a 12- x 8- x 2-inch baking dish. Place dish in a 13- x 9- x 2-inch baking pan; pour hot water into pan to a depth of 1 inch. Bake at 300° for 1 hour and 10 minutes or until a knife inserted between center and edge comes out clean. Remove baking dish from pan of water immediately. Cool to room temperature. Cover, and chill.

Just before serving, place custard in a 13- x 9- x 2-inch baking pan filled with ice. Sift light brown sugar evenly over custard. Broil 3 to 4 inches from heating element 2 minutes or until sugar melts and is caramelized. Remove custard from pan of ice. Spoon into individual serving bowls. Yield: 8 to 10 servings.

CARAMEL FLAN

1⅓ cups sugar, divided
⅓ cup boiling water
3 cups milk, scalded
5 eggs, beaten
¼ teaspoon salt
½ teaspoon vanilla extract

Sprinkle 1 cup sugar evenly into a 10-inch cast-iron skillet; place over low heat, and cook, stirring constantly with a wooden spoon, until sugar melts and becomes a light golden brown. Gradually add boiling water, stirring to make a smooth syrup. Remove from heat, and carefully pour hot caramelized syrup into an oven-proof 5½-cup ring mold.

Using oven mitts to grasp edges of mold, carefully tilt mold to coat sides with caramelized syrup. Set aside to cool.

Combine milk, remaining sugar, eggs, salt, and vanilla in a medium mixing bowl; beat well with a wire whisk. Slowly pour custard mixture into prepared mold, being careful not to disturb the caramelized syrup in bottom of mold.

Place mold in a 13- x 9- x 2-inch baking pan. Add warm water to a depth of 1 inch. Bake at 350° for 45 minutes or until a knife inserted in custard near edge of mold comes out clean. Transfer mold immediately to a pan of cold water; allow custard to cool completely. Remove mold from water, and chill thoroughly in refrigerator.

Carefully run a knife around edges of custard. Invert custard onto a serving platter, and unmold. Slice and serve. Yield: 8 to 10 servings.

Caramel Flan, fit for a Spanish grandee, cooks in a pan coated with melted sugar. Ah, so good!

CARAMEL CUSTARD PETIT ARNAUD

1¾ cups sugar, divided
4 eggs, lightly beaten
2 cups warm milk (105°
  to 115°)
1 teaspoon vanilla extract

Sprinkle ¾ cup sugar evenly into a 10-inch cast-iron skillet; place over medium heat, and cook, stirring constantly with a wooden spoon, until sugar melts and becomes a light golden brown. Pour caramelized sugar into six 6-ounce custard cups or ramekins. Set aside.

Combine remaining sugar and eggs in a medium mixing bowl, beating well; gradually add milk, stirring constantly. Stir in vanilla, and pour into prepared custard cups.

Place custard cups in a 13- x 9- x 2-inch baking pan; pour hot water into pan to a depth of 1 inch. Bake at 325° for 1½ hours or until a knife inserted halfway between center and edge of custard comes out clean. Remove cups from water; cool. Invert custard onto individual dessert plates. Serve warm or chilled. Yield: 6 servings.

From the village of Bosdarros, France, Count Arnaud Cazenave came to America to study medicine in the 1800s. Fortunately for the gourmands of the South, he settled in New Orleans. He opened a café in the Old Absinthe House in order to remain in the city. In 1811, he opened his restaurant at 811 Bienville Street. The magic of Arnaud's famous restaurant is still at work today. A trip to New Orleans would not be complete without a luncheon of Coquilles Saint Jacques or Shrimp Arnaud and a Caramel Custard Petit Arnaud. As the good Count put it, "The Art of Cooking is an art to be proud of. It is the soul of festivity at all times and to all ages."

The French country style of Arnaud's is an appropriate setting for their continental cuisine.

FRIED CUSTARD

4 cups milk
3 (3½-inch) sticks
  cinnamon
¼ teaspoon baking soda
1 cup sugar
½ cup cornstarch
¼ cup all-purpose flour
6 egg yolks
1 tablespoon butter or
  margarine, softened
1½ teaspoons vanilla extract
Pinch of salt
3 egg whites, beaten
2 cups cracker meal
Vegetable oil
Sifted powdered sugar

Combine milk, cinnamon, and soda in a heavy saucepan; cook over medium heat until candy thermometer registers 160°. Discard cinnamon sticks.

Combine sugar, cornstarch, and flour in a large saucepan; gradually stir in scalded milk mixture. Cook over medium heat, stirring constantly, until mixture is thickened and bubbly. Remove from heat.

Beat yolks in a medium mixing bowl until thick and lemon colored. Gradually stir one-fourth of hot mixture into yolks; add to remaining hot mixture, stirring constantly. Cook over medium heat, stirring constantly with a metal spoon, 2 minutes or until mixture coats the spoon. Remove from heat. Add butter, vanilla, and salt; stir until butter melts.

Pour custard into a greased 13- x 9- x 2-inch baking pan. Cool completely. Cover tightly, and place in freezer overnight.

Cut custard into 1½-inch squares. Dip squares in beaten egg whites; dredge in cracker meal. Fry in deep hot oil (375°) until golden brown. Drain well on paper towels. Sprinkle with powdered sugar. Serve hot. Yield: 12 servings.

Watts, Wohl, and Associates

Pots de Crème au Chocolat are garnished with dainty twists of candied orange peel.

PETITS POTS DE CRÈME AU CAFÉ

6 egg yolks, beaten
½ cup sugar
⅛ teaspoon salt
2 cups half-and-half, scalded
1½ teaspoons instant coffee
  granules
1½ teaspoons vanilla extract
Whipped cream

Combine egg yolks, sugar, and salt in a mixing bowl; stir well. Gradually add half-and-half, stirring constantly. Stir in coffee and vanilla.

Pour mixture evenly into six 4-ounce ovenproof pots de crème or custard cups; cover. Place cups in a 13- x 9- x 2-inch baking pan; add hot water to a depth of 1 inch.

Bake at 325° for 30 minutes or until a knife inserted between center and edge comes out clean. Remove cups from pan; cool to room temperature. Chill. Top with whipped cream. Yield: 6 servings.

POTS DE CRÈME AU CHOCOLAT

½ cup sugar
3 tablespoons cocoa
1 teaspoon grated orange rind
¾ cup whipping cream
4 egg yolks
Sweetened whipped cream
Candied orange peel

Combine sugar, cocoa, and orange rind in top of a double boiler; gradually add whipping cream, stirring until smooth. Cook over simmering water until sugar dissolves and mixture is smooth.

Beat egg yolks well with a wire whisk. Gradually stir one-fourth of chocolate mixture into yolks; quickly add to remaining chocolate mixture, stirring constantly. Cook over boiling water until thickened. Cool.

Spoon mixture into 4 cordial glasses or demitasse cups. Chill. Garnish with sweetened whipped cream and orange peel. Yield: 4 servings.

DIXIE CHOCOLATE SOUFFLÉ

1 cup sugar
½ cup cocoa
2½ tablespoons all-purpose
  flour
⅛ teaspoon salt
½ cup milk, scalded
¼ cup butter or margarine,
  melted
3 eggs, separated
1 teaspoon vanilla
  extract
Sweetened whipped
  cream

Combine sugar, cocoa, flour, and salt in top of a double boiler; gradually stir in scalded milk and butter. Place over boiling water, and cook, stirring constantly, 8 minutes or until mixture is thickened.

Beat egg yolks in a small mixing bowl. Gradually stir one-fourth of hot cocoa mixture into yolks; add to remaining hot cocoa mixture, stirring constantly. Remove from heat, and stir in vanilla; let cool to room temperature.

Beat egg whites (at room temperature) until stiff peaks form; gently fold beaten egg whites into cooled cocoa mixture.

Pour into a lightly greased 1-quart soufflé dish. Place dish in a 13- x 9- x 2-inch baking pan; pour hot water into pan to a depth of 1 inch. Bake at 350° for 50 minutes or until puffed and firm. Spoon into individual serving bowls; serve immediately with sweetened whipped cream. Yield: 6 servings.

BLUEBERRY SOUFFLÉ

2 cups frozen blueberries,
  thawed
1 cup sugar
3 tablespoons water
1 teaspoon lemon juice
7 egg whites
½ teaspoon grated lemon rind
Blueberry Sauce

Lightly oil a 3-quart soufflé dish; sprinkle with sugar.

Cut a piece of aluminum foil long enough to fit around soufflé dish, allowing a 1-inch overlap; fold foil lengthwise into thirds. Lightly oil one side of foil; wrap around outside of dish, oiled side against dish, allowing foil to extend 3 inches above rim to form a collar. Secure foil around dish with string or freezer tape.

Process blueberries through a food mill or sieve; reserve liquid, and discard pulp. Combine blueberry liquid, sugar, water, and lemon juice in a large saucepan; cook over low heat, stirring constantly, until sugar dissolves. Cook over medium heat, without stirring, until mixture reaches thread stage (234°). Remove from heat; cool.

Beat egg whites (at room temperature) until stiff peaks form. Add lemon rind. Fold a small amount of beaten egg white into blueberry mixture to aerate or lighten the mixture. Gently fold remaining beaten egg white into blueberry mixture. Spoon into prepared soufflé dish.

Bake at 400° for 25 minutes or until puffed and set. Spoon into individual serving bowls, and serve immediately with Blueberry Sauce. Yield: 8 to 10 servings.

1910 greeting card with chestnuts as symbols of good luck.

The chestnut is said to
    bring luck in the fall,
But Good Luck the year round
    is no "chestnut" at all.

Blueberry Sauce:

⅓ cup sugar
1½ tablespoons all-purpose
  flour
¼ teaspoon salt
1 cup hot water
1 tablespoon lemon juice
1 cup fresh or frozen
  blueberries, thawed and
  drained
2 tablespoons butter or
  margarine, softened

Combine sugar, flour, and salt in a small saucepan. Gradually add hot water and lemon juice, stirring until combined. Cook over medium heat, stirring constantly, until smooth and thickened. Stir in blueberries, and cook 2 to 3 additional minutes. Remove from heat; add butter, and stir until butter melts. Serve warm over soufflé. Yield: 1½ cups.

CHESTNUT SOUFFLÉ

4 eggs, separated
½ cup sugar
1 tablespoon butter or
  margarine, melted
1 tablespoon rum
1 teaspoon vanilla extract
Pinch of salt
1 cup cooked, ground
  chestnuts
½ cup whipping cream
1 tablespoon sugar
1 teaspoon rum

Cut a piece of aluminum foil long enough to fit around a 1-quart soufflé dish, allowing a 1-inch overlap; fold foil lengthwise into thirds. Lightly oil one side of foil and bottom of dish; wrap foil around outside of dish, oiled side against dish, allowing foil to extend 3 inches above rim to form a collar. Secure foil with string or freezer tape.

Beat egg yolks until thick and lemon colored. Add ½ cup sugar, butter, 1 tablespoon rum, vanilla, and salt; beat well. Stir in chestnuts.

Beat egg whites (at room temperature) until soft peaks form. Fold into chestnut mixture. Spoon into prepared soufflé dish. Place dish in a 13- x 9- x 2-inch baking pan; pour hot water into pan to a depth of 1 inch. Bake at 350° for 50 minutes or until puffed and set.

Beat whipping cream in a small mixing bowl until foamy; gradually add 1 tablespoon sugar, beating until soft peaks form. Beat in 1 teaspoon rum.

Spoon hot soufflé into individual serving bowls. Serve immediately with whipped cream topping. Yield: 6 servings.

Hot Lemon Soufflé, fresh from the oven and ready for a sprinkling of sliced sweetened strawberries.

HOT LEMON SOUFFLÉ

4 eggs, separated
1 cup sugar, divided
Grated rind and juice of 1
  lemon
⅛ teaspoon salt
Sifted powdered sugar
2 cups sliced sweetened
  strawberries

Lightly oil a 1½-quart soufflé dish; sprinkle with sugar.

Cut a piece of aluminum foil long enough to fit around soufflé dish, allowing a 1-inch overlap; fold foil lengthwise into thirds. Lightly oil one side of foil; wrap foil around outside of dish, oiled side against dish, allowing foil to extend 3 inches above rim to form a collar. Secure foil with freezer tape or string.

Beat yolks in a large mixing bowl until thick and lemon colored. Gradually add ½ cup sugar, lemon rind and juice, beating well; set aside.

Beat egg whites (at room temperature) until foamy. Gradually add salt and remaining ½ cup sugar, beating until stiff peaks form. Fold whites into lemon mixture, and spoon into prepared soufflé dish. Place dish in a 13- x 9- x 2-inch baking pan; pour hot water into pan to a depth of 1 inch. Bake at 350° for 1 hour or until puffed and set.

Dust top of soufflé with powdered sugar. Spoon into individual serving bowls; top with strawberries. Serve immediately. Yield: 6 servings.

FROM ICEBOX TO TABLE

It may surprise us that 200 years before Jello, cooks had access to molds in which to form gelled mixtures, but proof exists in extant household inventories of several mid-eighteenth-century estates. Tin, copper, and pewter molds were in common use. In 1776, Balfour & Barraus of Norfolk advertised for sale " . . . fluted moulds for blomange harlequins, eggs, stars, hedgehogs, fish, half moons, steeples, swans, obelisks, hens and chickens, packs of cards, and sunflowers &c. &c. for blomange, and all other sorts of tinware. . . . "

Molded jellies were popular and ornamental, served on the glass pyramids that came into vogue during Washington's administration. Colorful jellies made with isinglass, hartshorn, or calves' (or pigs' or sheep's) feet could be made in myriad shapes, making the newly elevated centerpiece come brilliantly alive. However, some of the old recipes suggested putting the jellies in glasses, and then placing the glasses on the pyramid, thus answering our question, "How did they keep them from melting in the hot, humid South in summer?" For winter entertaining, unmolded gels would doubtless have kept their form.

The Colonial flummery, either a custard or blancmange depending upon the thickening used, was chilled and unmolded for serving. We may have lost the word, but not the taste for the cooling, soothing smoothness to be found in its many descendants; this chapter is full of them.

In the mousse and the cold soufflé, mixtures supported by gelatin and aerated with whipped cream and/or egg white, we look for signs of French ancestry. And find it, even behind the legendary Greenbrier Cold Bourbon Soufflé. Note, too, the bavarian creams; they are the French *bavarois*.

Worth noting in making aerated cold molded desserts: Chill well and re-fold once or twice while still in the mixing bowl. Otherwise the airy part will float to the top and the mold will seem to have been made in two layers. Too, chilling dilutes flavor; err on the side of intensity.

Here are the elegant cool ones.

Orange Charlotte (front) presents itself like a jeweled crown. Strawberry Mousse from a shapely mold looks regal. Chocolate Mousse reigns in stemmed glasses.

MOLDED DELIGHTS

WINE JELLY MOLD

- 2 envelopes unflavored gelatin
- 1 cup water, divided
- ½ cup sugar
- 2 tablespoons lemon juice
- 1¼ cups sherry
- 1¼ cups port wine
- 1 apple, unpeeled, cored, and sliced
- 1 orange, peeled and sectioned
- 1 pear, unpeeled, cored, and sliced
- 1 cup sliced fresh strawberries
- 1 cup green seedless grapes
- Custard Sauce

Soften gelatin in ¼ cup water. Combine remaining water and sugar in a heavy saucepan; bring to a boil. Remove mixture from heat; add softened gelatin, stirring until gelatin dissolves. Stir in lemon juice, sherry, and wine, mixing well.

Pour gelatin mixture into a lightly greased 4-cup mold, and refrigerate overnight.

Unmold jelly onto a serving plate; arrange fruit around jelly. Slice and serve with Custard Sauce. Yield: 12 to 15 servings.

Custard Sauce:

- 3 egg yolks
- ½ cup sugar
- 2 cups milk, scalded
- 1 cup whipping cream
- 1 teaspoon vanilla extract

Combine egg yolks and sugar in top of a double boiler, beating well. Gradually add scalded milk, stirring constantly. Cook over boiling water, stirring constantly with a metal spoon, 20 minutes or until mixture coats the spoon. Remove from heat; cool to room temperature. Chill thoroughly.

Beat whipping cream until soft peaks form. Fold into chilled custard mixture; fold in vanilla. Cover and refrigerate 2 hours. Yield: 5 cups.

Rennet, obtained from the stomach of a calf, was (and is still) a useful and digestible jelling agent. It makes an uncooked blancmange, not a true custard; Mary Randolph called it a slip. Mrs. Porter gave this recipe for "Cup Custard, Not cooked . . . One quart of new milk, one pint of cream, four ounces of powdered loaf sugar, three tablespoonsful of wine in which rennet has been soaked; mix the milk, cream and sugar, and stir in the wine. Then pour into custard-cups, and set away till it becomes a curd; grate nutmeg on top, and eat with cream when cold."

The Enterprise Fruit, Wine, and Jelly Press, 1895, American gadgetry at its best.

Dessert Victorian style: New Cyclopaedia of Domestic Economy, *1872.*

STRAWBERRY BAVARIAN CREAM

2 envelopes unflavored
  gelatin
½ cup cold water
1 pint fresh strawberries,
  washed, hulled, and
  mashed
½ cup sugar
2 cups whipping cream,
  whipped
1 cup sliced strawberries
  (optional)

Combine gelatin and water in top of a double boiler; let stand 5 minutes or until softened. Cook over boiling water, stirring constantly, 1 minute or until gelatin dissolves. Remove from heat, and set aside to cool.

Combine mashed strawberries and sugar in a large mixing bowl. Add dissolved gelatin; mix well. Chill until consistency of unbeaten egg white.

Beat mixture until frothy and light pink in color. Fold in whipped cream, and pour into a lightly oiled 6-cup mold. Chill until firm. Unmold onto a serving plate, and garnish with sliced strawberries, if desired. Spoon into individual serving bowls to serve. Yield: 8 servings.

PEPPERMINT BAVARIAN

2 envelopes unflavored
  gelatin
½ cup cold water
2 cups milk
1 (12-ounce) package
  peppermint candy,
  crushed
Pinch of salt
1 cup whipping cream,
  whipped
Additional crushed
  peppermint candy

Soften gelatin in cold water; let stand 5 minutes.

Combine milk, 12 ounces crushed peppermint candy, and salt in top of a double boiler; place over boiling water, and cook until candy melts. Add softened gelatin, and stir until gelatin dissolves. Remove from heat. Transfer mixture to a large mixing bowl, and chill until consistency of unbeaten egg whites. Beat until light and fluffy.

Fold in whipped cream, and pour mixture into a lightly oiled 5½-cup mold. Chill overnight.

Unmold onto a serving platter, and garnish with additional crushed peppermint. Spoon into individual serving bowls. Yield: 6 to 8 servings.

RUM BAVARIAN CREAM

2 envelopes unflavored
   gelatin
½ cup cold water
4 eggs, separated
½ cup sugar
1½ cups milk, scalded
1 cup ground walnuts
⅓ cup light rum
2 cups whipping cream,
   divided
Grated chocolate

Soften gelatin in cold water; let stand 5 minutes.

Beat egg yolks in top of a double boiler until thick and lemon colored; gradually add sugar, beating well. Set aside.

Combine gelatin and milk; stir until gelatin dissolves. Gradually add milk mixture to egg mixture in double boiler, stirring constantly with a metal spoon. Cook over boiling water until mixture thickens and coats the spoon. Cool to room temperature. Stir in walnuts and rum. Transfer to a medium mixing bowl.

Beat 1 cup whipping cream until soft peaks form. Fold into gelatin mixture. Spoon into a lightly greased 6-cup mold. Chill overnight or until firm.

Unmold onto a serving platter. Beat remaining whipping cream until soft peaks form; spoon over mold, and sprinkle with chocolate. Spoon into individual serving dishes. Yield: 8 servings.

Coffee Bavarian topped with crushed peanut brittle.

COFFEE BAVARIAN

2 envelopes unflavored
   gelatin
1 cup milk
1 cup boiling, strong
   coffee
1 cup sugar
2 egg whites
⅛ teaspoon salt
2 cups whipping cream,
   whipped
Crushed peanut brittle

Soften gelatin in milk in a large mixing bowl. Add coffee and sugar, stirring until gelatin and sugar dissolve. Chill until mixture is consistency of unbeaten egg whites.

Beat egg whites (at room temperature) and salt until stiff peaks form. Fold beaten egg whites into chilled coffee mixture. Fold in whipped cream, and spoon mixture into a lightly oiled 9-cup ring mold. Chill until firm. Unmold and sprinkle with crushed peanut brittle. Slice; serve immediately. Yield: 10 to 12 servings.

CHESTNUT CREAM

1 envelope unflavored
  gelatin
¼ cup cold water
½ cup sugar
3 egg yolks
1½ cups milk, scalded
1 tablespoon sherry
½ cup cooked, ground
  chestnuts
Whipped cream (optional)

Soften gelatin in water; set aside. Combine sugar and egg yolks in a medium saucepan, stirring well. Gradually add milk, stirring until smooth. Cook over medium heat, stirring constantly, until mixture is slightly thickened. Remove from heat, and stir in softened gelatin and sherry. Chill until consistency of unbeaten egg whites.

Fold chestnuts into chilled custard mixture, and pour into a lightly greased 2½-cup mold. Refrigerate overnight.

Unmold onto a small serving platter, and top with whipped cream, if desired. Spoon into individual serving dishes. Yield: 6 servings.

Custards

Bonnie Slotnick

ORANGE CUSTARD CREAM

2 envelopes unflavored
  gelatin
½ cup cold water
2 cups milk
1 cup sugar
3 egg yolks, beaten
1 tablespoon grated
  orange rind
1 cup orange juice
Grated rind and juice
  of 1 lemon
½ cup whipping cream
Whipped cream
Orange twists

Soften gelatin in water, and set aside.

Combine milk and sugar in a heavy saucepan; stir until sugar dissolves. Cook, stirring frequently, over medium heat until candy thermometer registers 180°. Remove from heat; stir in softened gelatin.

Gradually stir one-fourth of hot milk mixture into beaten egg yolks; add to remaining hot milk mixture, stirring constantly. Stir in orange and lemon rind and juice. Chill until mixture is consistency of unbeaten egg whites.

Beat ½ cup whipping cream until soft peaks form; fold into orange mixture. Spoon into a lightly oiled 6-cup mold. Chill until set.

Unmold onto a serving platter, and garnish with whipped cream and orange twists. Spoon into individual serving bowls. Yield: 8 servings.

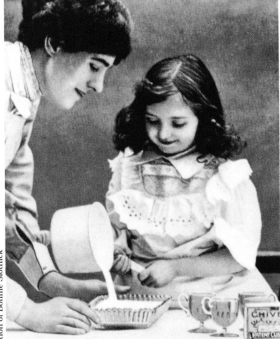

The ease of molding desserts, pictured in a booklet from Chivers Jelly, c.1906.

COCONUT CREAM WITH CARAMEL SAUCE

2 envelopes unflavored
  gelatin
½ cup cold milk
¾ cup milk, scalded
1 cup sugar
Pinch of salt
2 cups grated fresh coconut
1½ teaspoons vanilla extract
2 cups whipping cream
Caramel Sauce

Combine gelatin and cold milk; set aside to soften.

Combine scalded milk and sugar in a large mixing bowl; stir until sugar dissolves. Add gelatin mixture to hot mixture, stirring until gelatin dissolves. Add salt. Cool to consistency of unbeaten egg whites. Stir in coconut and vanilla.

Beat whipping cream until soft peaks form. Fold whipped cream into cooled gelatin mixture. Pour into a lightly oiled 9-cup mold, and chill overnight.

Unmold onto a serving platter. Spoon into serving bowls, and serve with hot Caramel Sauce. Yield: 10 to 12 servings.

Caramel Sauce:

1 cup firmly packed light
  brown sugar
1 cup sugar
1 tablespoon all-purpose flour
1 cup half-and-half
1 tablespoon butter or
  margarine

Combine first 3 ingredients in a large saucepan; stir well. Add remaining ingredients; bring to a boil. Reduce heat, and cook 10 minutes or until mixture thickens. Serve hot over Coconut Cream. Yield: 2 cups.

Irresistible creams: Coconut Cream with Caramel Sauce (front) and Filbert Cream with Apricot Sauce.

FILBERT CREAM WITH APRICOT SAUCE

2 egg yolks
¾ cup sugar
1 envelope unflavored
  gelatin
¼ cup cold milk
1¾ cups milk, scalded
½ cup ground filberts
2 tablespoons brandy
1 cup whipping cream
Apricot Sauce

Combine egg yolks and sugar in top of a double boiler; beat well. Soften gelatin in cold milk; stir into scalded milk. Gradually add milk mixture to egg mixture in top of double boiler, stirring constantly. Cook over boiling water, stirring frequently, 15 minutes or until mixture thickens slightly. Remove from heat. Let cool completely. Stir in nuts and brandy.

Beat 1 cup whipping cream until soft peaks form. Fold whipped cream into cooled gelatin mixture. Spoon mixture into a 1-quart fluted mold. Refrigerate overnight or until set.

Unmold onto a serving platter; serve with Apricot Sauce. Yield: 8 servings.

Apricot Sauce:

½ (6-ounce) package dried
  apricots
3 tablespoons sugar
1 tablespoon butter or
  margarine
1 tablespoon brandy

Combine apricots and water to cover in a heavy saucepan. Bring to a boil. Reduce heat; cover and simmer 30 mintues. Drain apricots, reserving ½ cup liquid.

Place drained apricots in container of an electric blender, and process until smooth. Return pureed apricots to saucepan; stir in sugar, butter, and reserved apricot liquid. Cook over low heat, stirring constantly, until mixture comes to a boil. Remove from heat, and stir in brandy. Serve sauce warm. Yield: 1 cup.

HONEY FLUMMERY

2 egg yolks
2 cups milk
2 envelopes unflavored
  gelatin
½ cup honey
1 tablespoon sherry
1 cup whipping cream,
  whipped
1 large peach, peeled, seeded,
  and sliced
¼ cup honey
1 tablespoon lemon juice

Combine egg yolks and milk in a heavy saucepan; beat well with a wire whisk. Sprinkle gelatin over milk mixture to soften; stir in ½ cup honey. Add to milk mixture, mixing well. Cook over low heat, stirring constantly, until creamy and slightly thickened. Remove from heat; stir in sherry. Transfer mixture to a large mixing bowl. Chill until consistency of unbeaten egg whites.

Fold whipped cream into gelatin mixture, and pour into a lightly oiled 5½-cup ring mold. Chill overnight.

Unmold onto a serving platter. Toss peach slices with ¼ cup honey and lemon juice. Arrange peach slices in center of mold; top each serving with peaches. Yield: 6 to 8 servings.

Collection of Business Americana

SNOW PUDDING

1 tablespoon unflavored
  gelatin
¼ cup cold water
1 cup boiling water
1 cup sugar
1 teaspoon grated lemon rind
¼ cup plus 1 tablespoon
  lemon juice
3 egg whites
Fresh whole strawberries
Custard Sauce

Soften gelatin in cold water in a medium mixing bowl; add boiling water; stir until gelatin dissolves. Add sugar, and stir until sugar dissolves. Let cool 15 minutes. Stir in lemon rind and juice. Chill until consistency of unbeaten egg whites.

Beat egg whites (at room temperature) until soft peaks form. Gently fold into lemon mixture. Spoon into a 1-quart serving dish, and refrigerate until firm.

Garnish pudding with strawberries. Spoon pudding into individual serving bowls, and serve with chilled Custard Sauce. Yield: 6 servings.

Custard Sauce:

1⅓ cups milk
2 egg yolks, beaten
2½ tablespoons sugar
Dash of salt
¼ teaspoon vanilla extract

Combine milk, egg yolks, sugar, and salt in a small saucepan; stir well. Cook over low heat, stirring constantly, until slightly thickened. Remove from heat, and stir in vanilla. Cool custard to room temperature; chill. Yield: about 1⅓ cups.

BLANCMANGE WITH STRAWBERRIES

1 quart strawberries, washed,
  hulled, and sliced
3 tablespoons sugar
3 tablespoons rum,
  divided
½ cup milk
½ cup whipping cream
¼ cup cold water
1 envelope unflavored
  gelatin
1 cup blanched whole
  almonds
2 cups water
½ cup sugar

Combine strawberries, 3 tablespoons sugar, and 2 tablespoons rum in a medium bowl. Mix well; cover and chill.

Combine milk, whipping cream, ¼ cup cold water, and gelatin in a medium saucepan; mix well. Let stand 5 minutes.

Place whole almonds in container of an electric blender; gradually add 2 cups water, and process until almonds are finely ground and liquid is milky. Squeeze almonds through cheesecloth to extract liquid. Discard almonds.

Add almond liquid and remaining ½ cup sugar to milk mixture in saucepan. Cook over low heat, stirring constantly, 4 minutes or until gelatin dissolves; stir in remaining rum.

Pour mixture into a well-greased 3-cup ring mold. Chill until firm. Unmold onto a serving plate, and serve with sweetened strawberries mixture. Yield: 6 servings.

MACAROON PUDDING

4 cups milk, divided
1½ cups sugar, divided
6 eggs, separated
2 tablespoons unflavored
  gelatin
1 dozen almond macaroons,
  crushed
Sliced almonds

Scald 3½ cups milk in top of a double boiler; gradually stir in 1¼ cups sugar. Beat egg yolks until thick and lemon colored. Stir a small amount of hot milk mixture into egg yolks; add to remaining hot milk mixture. Cook, stirring constantly with a metal spoon, until mixture thickens and coats the spoon. Remove from heat.

Soften gelatin in remaining milk; add softened gelatin and crushed macaroons to hot milk mixture; stir well. Chill until consistency of unbeaten egg whites.

Beat egg whites (at room temperature) until soft peaks form. Gradually add remaining ¼ cup sugar, beating until stiff peaks form. Fold egg whites into gelatin mixture, and spoon into a lightly oiled 8-cup mold. Chill overnight.

Unmold pudding onto a serving platter, and garnish with sliced almonds. Spoon into individual serving bowls. Yield: 10 to 12 servings.

*The good life,
reminiscent of F.
Scott Fitzgerald, c.1926.*

NESSELRODE PUDDING

2 cups milk
½ cup sugar
2 tablespoons vanilla extract
5 eggs, separated
2 cups almond macaroon
   crumbs
¾ cup raisins
28 whole blanched almonds,
   chopped
2 envelopes unflavored
   gelatin
¼ cup water
Sweetened whipped cream

Combine milk, sugar, and vanilla in top of a double boiler; place over boiling water, and cook until sugar dissolves. Beat egg yolks until thick and lemon colored. Stir a small amount of hot milk mixture into egg yolks; add to remaining hot milk mixture. Cook, stirring constantly with a metal spoon, until mixture thickens and coats the spoon. Remove from heat, and cool completely.

Add 2 cups macaroon crumbs, raisins, and chopped almonds to cooled mixture; stir well. Dissolve gelatin in water, and add to macaroon mixture; mix well. Chill until mixture is consistency of unbeaten egg whites.

Beat egg whites (at room temperature) until stiff peaks form. Gently fold beaten egg whites into gelatin mixture. Spoon into a lightly oiled 6½-cup mold, and chill overnight.

Unmold pudding onto a serving platter. Spoon into individual serving bowls, and serve with a dollop of sweetened whipped cream. Yield: 8 to 10 servings.

This Westinghouse refrigerator model sold for $180 in 1931.

CHOCOLATE MOUSSE

3 (1-ounce) squares
  unsweetened chocolate
⅓ cup milk chocolate
  morsels
½ cup hot water
¼ teaspoon vanilla extract
Pinch of salt
3 eggs, separated
¼ cup sugar
1½ cups whipping cream,
  whipped
Sweetened whipped cream
Chocolate curls

Combine chocolate, water, vanilla, and salt in top of a double boiler. Cook over boiling water, stirring constantly, until chocolate melts.

Beat egg yolks in a small mixing bowl until thick and lemon colored. Gradually stir one-fourth of hot chocolate mixture into egg yolks; add to remaining hot chocolate mixture, stirring constantly. Continue cooking, stirring constantly, 2 minutes or until mixture thickens. Set aside to cool.

Beat egg whites (at room temperature) in a medium mixing bowl until soft peaks form. Gradually add ¼ cup sugar, 1 tablespoon at a time, beating until peaks are stiff and glossy. Fold meringue and 1½ cups whipped cream into cooled chocolate mixture. Pour into ten 6-ounce stemmed glasses, and refrigerate until set. Garnish each mousse with sweetened whipped cream and chocolate curls before serving. Yield: 10 servings.

COFFEE MOUSSE

1 cup hot strong coffee
1 (10-ounce) package large
  marshmallows
1 teaspoon vanilla extract
1 cup whipping cream,
  whipped
Sliced almonds, toasted

Combine coffee and marsh-mallows in top of a double boiler. Cook over boiling water, stirring constantly, until marshmallows melt. Remove from heat; cool to room temperature. Chill to consistency of unbeaten egg whites. Add vanilla, and stir well.

Fold whipped cream into coffee mixture. Spoon into a lightly oiled 4-cup mold. Chill overnight. Unmold onto a serving plate, and garnish with almonds. Spoon onto individual serving plates. Yield: 8 servings.

SNOWDEN HOUSE
RUM MOUSSE

1½ dozen almond macaroons,
  broken into pieces
¼ cup butter or margarine,
  melted
2 envelopes unflavored
  gelatin
3 tablespoons cold water
1 cup light rum
6 egg yolks
1½ cups sugar, divided
2 cups whipping cream,
  divided
2 egg whites
2 tablespoons sugar
1 tablespoon light rum

Place macaroons on a baking sheet. Bake at 300° for 15 minutes or until lightly browned. Cool completely. Place macaroon pieces between two pieces of waxed paper; using a rolling pin, finely crush macaroons. Combine macaroon crumbs and butter in a small mixing bowl, stirring to blend well. Set aside ¼ cup crumb mixture. Place remaining mixture in a plastic wrap-lined 6½-cup ring mold. Press crumbs on bottom and halfway up sides of mold. Set mold aside.

Snowden House Rum Mousse takes its name from a historic home in Alexandria, Virginia. The 1790 house was built by Edgar Snowden, the son of the owner of the *Alexandria Gazette.* Old copies of this paper have provided researchers with invaluable "time capsules" of daily life in earlier days. Presidents have been entertained at Snowden House and Justice Hugo Black once owned it.

Soften gelatin in cold water; set aside. Place 1 cup rum in top of a double boiler. Heat over boiling water. Remove from heat. Add softened gelatin, stirring until gelatin dissolves. Cool completely.

Beat egg yolks in a medium mixing bowl until thick and lemon colored. Gradually add ½ cup sugar, beating constantly. Add cooled rum-gelatin mixture; beat well.

Beat 1 cup whipping cream until foamy. Gradually add ½ cup sugar, 1 tablespoon at a time, beating until soft peaks form. Fold into rum mixture.

Beat egg whites (at room temperature) until foamy. Gradually add remaining ½ cup sugar, 1 tablespoon at a time, beating until stiff peaks form. Fold into rum mixture. Spoon mixture into prepared mold. Cover and refrigerate overnight.

Beat remaining 1 cup whipping cream until foamy. Gradually add 2 tablespoons sugar and 1 tablespoon rum, beating until soft peaks form. Unmold mousse onto a serving platter. Garnish with whipped cream and reserved crumb mixture. Slice and serve immediately. Yield: 10 servings.

Front entrance of The Greenbrier, photographed in 1929.

THE GREENBRIER COLD BOURBON SOUFFLÉ

2 envelopes unflavored
  gelatin
1½ cups bourbon
16 eggs, separated
1 tablespoon plus 1 teaspoon
  vanilla extract
Pinch of salt
2 cups sugar
2 cups whipping cream,
  whipped
1 cup whipping cream,
  whipped
Toasted pecan halves
Toasted pecans, chopped

Cut a piece of aluminum foil long enough to fit around a 2-quart soufflé dish, allowing a 1-inch overlap. Fold foil lengthwise into thirds. Lightly oil one side of foil; wrap foil around outside of dish, oiled side against dish, allowing foil to extend 4 inches above rim to form a collar. Secure foil with string or freezer tape. Set aside.

Soften gelatin in bourbon in top of a double boiler. Cook over boiling water, stirring constantly, until gelatin dissolves.

Beat egg yolks in a large mixing bowl until thick and lemon colored. Combine eggs, bourbon mixture, and vanilla in top of a double boiler; mix well. Cook over boiling water, stirring constantly, until mixture thickens and coats a metal spoon. Cool to room temperature.

Beat egg whites (at room temperature) and salt in a large mixing bowl until foamy. Gradually add sugar, 1 tablespoon at a time, beating until mixture forms stiff glossy peaks.

Stir one-third of meringue into bourbon mixture with a wire whisk. Fold in remaining meringue and 2 cups whipped cream.

Spoon mixture into prepared soufflé dish; chill until set. Garnish with 1 cup whipped cream and toasted pecans. Spoon into individual serving bowls. Yield: 10 to 12 servings.

The Greenbrier Cold Bourbon Soufflé is only one of the exquisite foods that are a specialty at the famed resort.

STRAWBERRY DELIGHT

¾ cup sugar
1 tablespoon all-purpose
flour
1 envelope unflavored
gelatin
3 cups whipping cream
5 egg yolks, beaten
3 tablespoons brandy
1 teaspoon vanilla extract
Grated rind of 1 medium
orange
¾ cup strawberry puree
1 cup whipping cream,
whipped
1 pint strawberries, washed,
hulled, and halved
16 whole strawberries,
washed

Combine sugar, flour, and gelatin in a medium saucepan; add 3 cups whipping cream and egg yolks, stirring until smooth. Cook over medium heat, stirring constantly, 10 minutes. Remove from heat, and stir in brandy, vanilla, and grated orange rind. Chill until mixture is consistency of unbeaten egg whites.

Fold strawberry puree, 1 cup whipped cream, and strawberry halves into chilled mixture; spoon mixture into sixteen 5½-ounce parfait glasses. Chill completely, and garnish with whole strawberries. Yield: 16 servings.

TEXAS GRAPEFRUIT PARFAIT

4 Ruby Red grapefruit, halved
crosswise
1 envelope unflavored gelatin
½ cup plus 2 tablespoons
firmly packed brown sugar,
divided
2 cups half-and-half
1 teaspoon lemon juice
2 egg whites

Section grapefruit halves; set sections aside, and drain. Squeeze grapefruit halves, reserving ½ cup juice. Combine juice and gelatin in a small saucepan; let stand 1 minute. Cook over low heat, stirring constantly, until gelatin dissolves. Add ½ cup brown sugar, stirring until sugar dissolves.

Remove from heat. Stir in half-and-half and lemon juice. Chill thoroughly, stirring occasionally, until mixture begins to thicken.

Beat egg whites (at room temperature) until soft peaks form. Gradually add remaining brown sugar, beating until stiff peaks form. Fold into gelatin mixture. Spoon alternate layers of cream mixture and grapefruit sections into eight 6-ounce parfait glasses. Chill thoroughly. Yield: 8 servings.

CHARLOTTE RUSSE

1 envelope unflavored gelatin
3 tablespoons cold water
¼ cup sherry
1 tablespoon vanilla extract
1 cup whipping cream,
  whipped
2 egg whites
¼ cup sugar
10 ladyfingers, split
  lengthwise
Fresh fruit slices

Soften gelatin in cold water in top of a double boiler; cook over boiling water until gelatin dissolves. Add sherry and vanilla, mixing well. Cool to room temperature. Fold gelatin mixture into whipped cream. Set aside.

Beat egg whites (at room temperature) in a medium mixing bowl until soft peaks form. Gradually add sugar, 1 tablespoon at a time, and beat until stiff and glossy. Fold meringue into whipped cream mixture.

Line the sides of a 1½-quart serving bowl with ladyfingers. Pour in filling; chill until set. Garnish with fresh fruit slices, and spoon into individual serving bowls. Yield: 6 servings.

The Garland Stove Co.
made cooking look like
child's play in ad, c.1890.

APRICOT CHARLOTTE

1 (6-ounce) package dried
  apricots
1¼ cups sugar, divided
½ cup water
1 tablespoon cornstarch
½ cup cold milk
1 cup milk, scalded
2 eggs, separated
1 teaspoon vanilla extract
1 teaspoon lemon extract
½ cup whipping cream
3 (3-ounce) packages
  ladyfingers, split lengthwise
Sweetened whipped cream
Grated orange rind

Place apricots and water to cover in a medium saucepan. Bring to a boil. Reduce heat; cover and simmer 30 minutes. Drain well.

Place apricots in container of an electric blender; process until smooth. Return apricot puree to saucepan. Stir in ¾ cup sugar and ½ cup water. Bring to a boil, stirring until sugar dissolves. Remove from heat. Cool to room temperature. Chill thoroughly.

Combine remaining sugar and cornstarch in a heavy saucepan, stirring well. Stir in cold milk. Gradually add scalded milk, stirring constantly.

Beat egg yolks until thick and lemon colored. Gradually stir one-fourth of hot milk mixture into egg yolks; add to remaining hot milk mixture, stirring constantly. Return to low heat; cook, stirring constantly, until smooth and thickened. Remove from heat. Cool to room temperature. Stir in flavorings.

Beat egg whites (at room temperature) until soft peaks form. Fold into custard mixture. Chill thoroughly.

Beat whipping cream until soft peaks form. Fold into custard mixture.

Line bottom and sides of a lightly greased glass 2-quart soufflé or serving dish with split ladyfingers. Spoon half of custard mixture into dish; top with a layer of ladyfingers. Spread apricot mixture over ladyfingers; top with another layer of ladyfingers. Spoon remaining custard mixture over ladyfingers. Top with remaining ladyfingers. Cover and refrigerate overnight.

Top with sweetened whipped cream; sprinkle with grated orange rind. Spoon into individual serving dishes to serve. Yield: 10 servings.

Chocolate Charlotte may not cure a chocolate craving, but it certainly will allay it.

CHOCOLATE RUM CHARLOTTE

12 almond macaroons
¼ cup rum
16 (1-ounce) squares
   semisweet chocolate
¼ cup plus 2 tablespoons
   water
¼ cup plus 3 tablespoons
   sugar, divided
6 eggs, separated
3 (3-ounce) packages
   ladyfingers, split lengthwise
1 cup whipping cream,
   whipped
Grated chocolate

Combine macaroons and rum in a shallow dish. Set aside.

Combine chocolate, water, and ¼ cup plus 2 tablespoons sugar in top of a double boiler. Cook over boiling water until chocolate melts.

Beat egg yolks until thick and lemon colored. Gradually stir one-fourth of hot chocolate mixture into egg yolks; add to remaining hot chocolate mixture, stirring constantly. Remove from heat; cool to room temperature.

Beat egg whites (at room temperature) until foamy. Add remaining sugar, beating until stiff peaks form. Gently fold into chocolate mixture.

Line the bottom and sides of a 9-inch springform pan with ladyfingers. Spoon half the chocolate mixture into pan. Place macaroon mixture over chocolate mixture. Add remaining chocolate mixture; top with ladyfingers. Cover; refrigerate overnight.

Remove sides of pan; place charlotte on a serving platter. Top with whipped cream, and sprinkle with grated chocolate. Yield: 16 to 20 servings.

CHOCOLATE CHARLOTTE

32 ladyfingers, split
   lengthwise
3 (6-ounce) packages
   semisweet chocolate
   morsels
½ cup sugar, divided
⅓ cup water
1 teaspoon vanilla extract
8 eggs, separated
Sifted powdered sugar
Chocolate curls (optional)

Line bottom and sides of a 9-inch springform pan with ladyfingers; reserve remaining ladyfingers. Set aside.

Combine chocolate morsels, ¼ cup sugar, and water in top of a double boiler. Place over boiling water and cook, stirring constantly, until chocolate melts and sugar dissolves. Remove from heat, and stir in vanilla. Let cool to room temperature.

Beat egg yolks in a large mixing bowl until thick and lemon colored; gradually add chocolate mixture, beating constantly, until thickened.

Beat egg whites (at room temperature) until foamy. Gradually add remaining sugar, 1 tablespoon at a time, beating until stiff peaks form. Gently fold egg whites into chocolate mixture.

Alternate layers of chocolate mixture and ladyfingers in prepared springform pan, beginning and ending with chocolate mixture. Cover and refrigerate overnight.

Remove sides of springform pan; place charlotte on a serving platter. Sprinkle generously with powdered sugar; garnish with chocolate curls, if desired. Slice to serve. Yield: 16 to 20 servings.

A pretty girl poses next to a young orange tree in a Houston, Texas, orange grove, c.1905.

Harris County Heritage Society

STRAWBERRY CHARLOTTE

Sifted powdered sugar
32 ladyfingers, split
   lengthwise
2 tablespoons unflavored
   gelatin
¼ cup water
1 quart fresh strawberries,
   washed, hulled,
   and pureed
¾ cup sugar
2 cups whipping cream,
   whipped
Additional fresh strawberries,
   washed and halved

Sprinkle powdered sugar evenly over the smooth side of each ladyfinger half. Line the bottom and sides of a 9-inch springform pan with ladyfingers, reserving remaining ladyfingers. Set aside.

Soften gelatin in water; set aside. Combine pureed strawberries and sugar in a medium saucepan. Bring to a boil; add softened gelatin, stirring until well blended. Transfer to a large mixing bowl, and cool to room temperature. Chill until the consistency of unbeaten egg whites.

Gently fold whipped cream into chilled strawberry mixture. Alternate layers of strawberry mixture and ladyfingers in prepared springform pan, beginning and ending with strawberry mixture. Cover and chill thoroughly.

Remove sides of springform pan, and transfer charlotte to a chilled serving platter. Garnish with strawberry halves. Slice and serve immediately. Yield: 12 to 16 servings.

ORANGE CHARLOTTE

3 cups water, divided
1 cup sugar
1 envelope unflavored gelatin
1½ cups orange sections,
   divided
1 cup orange juice
¼ cup lemon juice
2 cups whipping cream
1 (6¼-ounce) package
   miniature marshmallows
1½ cups chopped pecans
3 (3-ounce) packages
   ladyfingers, split lengthwise
Grated coconut
Orange slices, halved

Combine 2 cups water and sugar in a medium saucepan; cook over low heat, stirring constantly, until sugar dissolves. Cook over high heat, without stirring, until mixture reaches soft ball stage (240°).

Soften gelatin in remaining water. Add to syrup mixture, stirring until gelatin dissolves. Cool to room temperature. Stir in 1 cup orange sections and juice. Chill to consistency of unbeaten egg whites.

Beat whipping cream and marshmallows until soft peaks form. Fold in pecans. Fold marshmallow mixture into orange mixture.

Line bottom and sides of a 9-inch springform pan with split ladyfingers. Spoon orange mixture into prepared pan. Cover and refrigerate overnight.

Remove sides of pan; place charlotte on a serving platter. Sprinkle top with coconut; garnish with remaining orange sections and orange slices. Yield: 16 to 20 servings.

Note: One (6¼-ounce) package miniature marshmallows is equivalent to ½ pound large marshmallows, chopped.

CHOCOLATE MINT CHARLOTTE

2 (3-ounce) packages
  ladyfingers, split lengthwise
2 (1-ounce) squares
  unsweetened chocolate
¼ cup plus 1 tablespoon
  sugar
¼ cup water
5 eggs, separated
½ teaspoon mint extract
1 cup whipping cream,
  whipped
Additional whipped cream
  (optional)

Line the bottom and sides of a
waxed paper-lined and greased
9-inch loafpan with ladyfingers,
reserving remaining lady-
fingers. Set aside.

Place chocolate squares in top
of a double boiler. Place over
boiling water; cook, stirring frequently, until chocolate melts.
Add sugar, water, and egg yolks;
cook, stirring constantly, until
mixture is smooth and thickened. Remove from heat, and
stir in mint extract. Cool mixture to room temperature.

Beat egg whites (at room temperature) until stiff peaks form.
Fold egg whites and 1 cup
whipped cream into chocolate
mixture; spoon into prepared
pan. Top with remaining ladyfingers. Cover; chill overnight.

Unmold cake onto a chilled
serving platter; frost with additional whipped cream, if desired. Slice and serve
immediately. Yield: 10 servings.

*A 1925 ad for
Shotwell's Marshmallows
shows many uses
of the confection.*

CHOCOLATE MARSHMALLOW ICEBOX DESSERT

½ pound vanilla wafers, finely
  crushed, and divided
½ cup butter or margarine,
  softened
½ cup commercial chocolate
  syrup
½ cup sifted powdered sugar
1 (6¼-ounce) package
  miniature marshmallows
1 cup chopped pecans
1 teaspoon vanilla extract
½ teaspoon salt
3 egg whites
Sweetened whipped cream

Spread half of vanilla wafer
crumbs in a 10- x 6- x 2-inch
baking dish. Set aside.

Combine butter, chocolate
syrup, and powdered sugar in a
large bowl; mix well. Stir in
marshmallows, pecans, vanilla,
and salt.

Beat egg whites (at room temperature) until soft peaks form.
Fold into marshmallow mixture.
Spread over vanilla wafer crumb
layer. Top with remaining vanilla wafer crumbs. Refrigerate
until thoroughly chilled or overnight. Top with sweetened
whipped cream; spoon into
serving dishes to serve. Yield: 8
servings.

Note: One 6¼-ounce package
miniature marshmallows is
equivalent to ½ pound large
marshmallows, chopped.

FAMOUS CHOCOLATE REFRIGERATOR ROLL

2 cups whipping cream
1 teaspoon vanilla extract
1 (8½-ounce) package
  chocolate wafers
Chocolate curls (optional)

Beat whipping cream in a medium mixing bowl until soft peaks form; add vanilla, and beat until well blended.

Spread whipped cream mixture on one side of wafers. Put wafers together in stacks of 4 to 5. On a serving platter, place stacks together to make a roll. Frost entire roll with remaining whipped cream mixture. Chill 4 to 6 hours. Garnish with chocolate curls, if desired.

Slice diagonally at a 45° angle, and serve on individual dessert plates. Yield: 12 servings.

ORANGE ICEBOX CAKE

2 envelopes unflavored
  gelatin
½ cup cold water
1½ cups sugar
1 cup orange juice
¼ cup lemon juice
1 (9-inch) commercial angel
  food cake
2 large oranges, peeled and
  sectioned
1 (10-ounce) package
  marshmallows, quartered
1 cup whipping cream,
  whipped
Sweetened whipped cream
Orange slices

Soften gelatin in water; set aside. Combine sugar and juices in a medium saucepan, stirring well. Bring to a boil; reduce heat and simmer, uncovered, 5 minutes. Add softened gelatin, stirring well. Chill until the consistency of unbeaten egg whites.

Slice angel food cake into ½-inch-thick slices. Line bottom and sides of a 9-inch loafpan with cake slices, reserving any remaining cake slices.

Add orange sections and marshmallows to chilled orange juice mixture. Gently fold in 1 cup whipped cream. Spoon mixture into prepared loafpan, and top with remaining cake slices. Cover and chill overnight.

Unmold cake onto a chilled serving platter. Garnish with sweetened whipped cream and orange slices. Yield: 10 servings.

PINEAPPLE ICEBOX CAKE

2 (20-ounce) cans pineapple
  tidbits
¼ cup sugar
½ cup butter or margarine,
  softened
1½ cups sifted powdered
  sugar
1 egg, beaten
48 vanilla wafers
½ cup chopped pecans
Whipped cream (optional)

Combine pineapple and sugar in a heavy saucepan; bring to a boil. Reduce heat; simmer 20 minutes or until liquid is absorbed. Set aside.

Cream butter; gradually add powdered sugar, beating well. Add egg; beat well. Stir into pineapple. Cook over low heat 2 minutes or until saucy.

Layer 16 vanilla wafers, half of sauce, and half the nuts in an 8-inch square baking dish. Repeat layers, ending with vanilla wafers. Cover with waxed paper. Place a weight over cake. Refrigerate overnight.

Spoon cake into individual serving dishes; top with whipped cream, if desired. Yield: 8 servings.

Nabisco, Inc.

Recipe on every tin of "Uneeda Bakers"
FAMOUS CHOCOLATE WAFERS
NATIONAL BISCUIT COMPANY

Decades ago, when the National Biscuit Company brought out "Famous Chocolate Wafers," there was a wonderful, simple recipe on the box that was eagerly welcomed by cooks all over the country. It consisted of nothing but the wafers, copious amounts of whipped cream, and some time in the refrigerator. (Frozen whipped topping was not mentioned as an option.) For years, it was not possible to attend a luncheon without eating it, artfully sliced on the bias. The recipe can still be found on some packages.

Strawberry Roulage: Fresh berries and cream rolled for slicing.

STRAWBERRY ROULAGE

¾ cup all-purpose flour
1 teaspoon baking powder
¼ teaspoon salt
4 eggs, separated
¾ cup sugar, divided
2 teaspoons water
1 teaspoon vanilla extract
½ cup sifted powdered sugar, divided
1½ cups whipping cream
3 cups sliced, fresh strawberries, divided

Sift together flour, baking powder, and salt. Set aside.

Beat egg whites (at room temperature) until foamy. Gradually add ¼ cup plus 2 tablespoons sugar, 1 tablespoon at a time, beating until stiff peaks form. Set aside.

Beat egg yolks in a large mixing bowl until thick and lemon colored. Gradually add remaining sugar, beating 5 minutes or until light and fluffy. Add water and vanilla; beat well. Fold egg whites into yolk mixture. Gradually fold in flour mixture, ¼ cup at a time, until well blended.

Pour batter evenly into a waxed paper-lined 15- x 10- x 1-inch jellyroll pan. Bake at 375° for 12 to 15 minutes.

Sift 2 tablespoons powdered sugar in a 15- x 10-inch rectangle on a linen towel. When cake is done, immediately loosen from sides of pan, and turn out onto powdered sugar. Peel off waxed paper. Starting at narrow end, roll up cake and towel together; let cool on a wire rack, seam side down.

Beat whipping cream until foamy; gradually add remaining powdered sugar, beating until soft peaks form.

Unroll cake, and remove towel. Spread with half of sweetened whipped cream. Top with 2 cups strawberries; re-roll cake. Spread outside of cake roll with remaining whipped cream. Garnish with remaining strawberries. Chill until serving time. Cut into slices to serve. Yield: 8 to 10 servings.

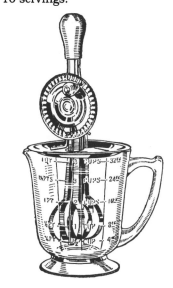

THE ICE CREAM PARLOR

S urely no one alive has been spared the story of Nero, who ate honey and wine on snow in the first century; his courtesans, reportedly, liked to hold ice in their mouths. Historians believe that the roots of ice cream are to be found much farther East. The word sherbet goes back to an Arabian word for drink. But it was the Italian traders who brought back the Middle Eastern know-how in the 1400s.

Catherine de Medici is credited with bringing sweet ices from Florence to France when she became Henri II's wife in the 1500s. Attempts were made to keep the recipe secret, but there was a breach in security; the common man would have ices too. By the mid-1600s, an entrepreneur had set up to sell ices, and soon Parisians were patronizing hundreds of ice and sherbet sellers. Helpfully, doctors prescribed ices for sickness, making for a fine year-round demand.

The hand-operated freezer came along in the mid-1800s. In 1851, ice cream was first made commercially in Baltimore, paving the way for today's mammoth industry. Chefs, housewives, and writers had been working with frozen desserts for over a century. English writers Hannah Glasse (*The Art of Cookery*, 1747) and Elizabeth Raffald (*English Housekeeper*, 1769) used two containers, one, with the base mixture, inside the other, which was filled with ice and salt. The "basons" were made of tin or pewter. Mary Randolph (*The Virginia Housewife*, 1824) observed that the cans should be tall and narrow, the outer tub only a few inches larger, in order not to waste the ice. And she insisted that the inner can should be turned constantly. There was no crank or paddle at that time.

Developments came quickly after Baltimore's pioneering of the commercial venture. We got Baked Alaska in 1867 to celebrate the purchase of Alaska from Russia, the ice cream soda in the 1870s, and the sundae around the turn of the century. Abe Doumar invented the ice cream cone at the St. Louis Exposition in 1904. Now over 300 flavors of ice cream can be identified, including, bless us, bubble gum.

Ice creams and sherbets, in or out of molds, store-bought or homemade, are always a favorite. Try, too, other frozen delights in freezer trays — this one made with pineapple topped with vanilla wafer crumbs.

WE ALL SCREAM . . .

CRANBERRY ICE

1½ cups fresh cranberries
3½ cups water, divided
1½ cups sugar, divided
⅔ cup orange juice
2 tablespoons lemon juice

Combine cranberries, ½ cup water, and ½ cup sugar in a medium saucepan; bring to a boil. Cook over medium heat 8 minutes, stirring frequently. Remove from heat, and cool slightly. Process cranberry mixture through a food mill; discard pulp, and reserve puree.

Combine cranberry puree, remaining water, sugar, and juice; stir until well blended. Pour cranberry mixture into two 2-cup metal ice trays (with dividers removed); freeze until ice crystals form around upper edge of ice trays. Remove from freezer; stir well, and return to freezer. Repeat procedure until mixture reaches the consistency of a sherbet. Scoop into sherbet dishes, and serve immediately. Yield: about 1 quart.

WINE ICE

1 cup water
1 cup sugar
2 teaspoons grated lemon rind
½ cup lemon juice
1 (25-ounce) bottle rosé

Combine water and sugar in a small saucepan; bring to a boil. Reduce heat and simmer 5 minutes, stirring occasionally; cool.

Combine syrup, rind, juice, and wine; pour into two 2-cup metal ice trays (with dividers removed). Freeze until almost firm. Spoon into a bowl; beat with an electric mixer until slushy. Freeze in trays until firm. Yield: 1 quart.

GRAPE ICE

⅔ cup sugar
1½ cups water
1 cup lemon juice
1 cup grape juice
¼ cup orange juice

Combine sugar and water in a heavy saucepan; bring to a boil, stirring frequently. Boil 5 minutes. Remove from heat, and add remaining ingredients, stirring well. Cool.

Pour juice mixture into two 2-cup metal ice trays (with dividers removed). Freeze until mixture reaches consistency of a sherbet, stirring occasionally during freezing. Scoop into sherbet dishes, and serve. Yield: about 1 quart.

Cranberry Ice may serve not only as a crisp-flavored light dessert, but also as a palate refresher in the midst of a multi-course dinner.

A 1903 co-op ad: J.A. Grasberger of Richmond, Virginia, made the ice company's wagon.

APRICOT SHERBET

2 (17-ounce) cans apricot
 halves, drained
Grated rind and juice of 3
 medium lemons
1 quart water
2 cups sugar
½ teaspoon almond extract
½ teaspoon vanilla extract
3 egg whites
1½ cups whipping cream,
 whipped

Combine apricots and lemon rind and juice in container of an electric blender; process until smooth. Set aside.

Bring water to a boil in a large saucepan; add sugar, and boil 1 minute. Remove from heat, and cool completely. Add flavorings.

Pour water mixture and apricot mixture into freezer can of a 2-quart hand-turned or electric freezer. Freeze according to manufacturer's instructions 5 minutes or until mixture thickens.

Beat egg whites (at room temperature) until stiff peaks form; fold into whipped cream. Fold whipped cream mixture into apricot mixture. Continue to freeze according to manufacturer's instructions. Let ripen at least 1 hour before serving. Scoop into sherbet dishes, and serve immediately. Yield: about 1 quart.

In the early 1800s, enterprising businessmen in the North recognized the need for ice in hot climates. They began harvesting blocks of ice in winter, packing them in sawdust, and shipping them not only to the Southern United States, but to places as far away as China and the Middle East. Fortunes were made in the ice trade. The mechanical freezing of ice brought the local ice man, and he flourished up until most people had changed to refrigerators by the 1930s. Ice cream became progressively more accessible.

Photographer: John O'Hagan

CRANBERRY SHERBET

1 (12-ounce) package fresh
  cranberries
½ teaspoon unflavored
  gelatin
1 cup cold water, divided
1 cup sugar
⅛ teaspoon salt
2 tablespoons lemon juice

Combine cranberries and water to cover in a heavy saucepan. Bring to a boil. Reduce heat; cover and simmer 15 minutes. Drain and cool. Process cranberries through a food mill. Discard pulp, and reserve puree.

Soften gelatin in ¼ cup water.

Combine cranberry puree, remaining water, sugar, and salt in a heavy saucepan. Bring to a boil, stirring constantly. Remove from heat; stir in softened gelatin and lemon juice. Cool.

Pour into a 2-cup metal ice tray (with divider removed); freeze for several hours, stirring 2 to 3 times during freezing process until mixture reaches the consistency of a sherbet.

Scoop into sherbet dishes; serve immediately. Yield: 1 pint.

Blackberry Sherbet: A taste treat with a zip of lemon.

BLACKBERRY SHERBET

2 (16-ounce) packages frozen
  blackberries, thawed and
  mashed
2 cups sugar, divided
1 envelope unflavored gelatin
½ cup boiling water
Juice of 2 medium lemons

Combine mashed berries and 1 cup sugar in a large mixing bowl. Set aside 1 hour.

Press blackberry mixture through a sieve; set blackberry juice aside, and discard pulp.

Dissolve gelatin in boiling water in a large mixing bowl; stir in blackberry juice. Add remaining sugar, lemon juice, and enough water to yield 5 cups of mixture.

Pour mixture into freezer can of a 1-gallon hand-turned or electric freezer. Freeze according to manufacturer's instructions. Let ripen 1½ to 2 hours before serving. Scoop into sherbet dishes, and serve immediately. Yield: 3 quarts.

Note: Two quarts fresh blackberries, mashed, may be substituted for frozen berries.

Don't gather 1st. snow, Mom always said. "It collects germs from air and is not safe for eating, but eat second snow and make ice cream." Mix a big pan of snow, put in sugar and vanilla . . . and rich sweet milk. It is delicious! And kids loved it!

Seems Like I Done It This A-Way

GRAPE SHERBET

½ cup lemon juice
1½ cups grape juice
1½ cups sugar
2 cups milk
1 cup half-and-half
Fresh grape clusters
  (optional)

Combine all ingredients except grape clusters in a large metal mixing bowl; mix well. Freeze until ice crystals form around upper edge of mixture. Remove from freezer, and beat well with an electric mixer. Return mixture to freezer. Repeat freezing procedure until mixture reaches the consistency of a sherbet. Spoon mixture into a 6-cup ice cream mold, and freeze overnight.

Unmold and garnish with grape clusters, if desired. Scoop into sherbet dishes, and serve immediately. Yield: 1½ quarts.

GRAPEFRUIT SHERBET

3 Ruby Red grapefruits,
  halved
1¼ cups sugar
⅓ cup water
3 egg whites
¼ teaspoon cream of tartar
Dash of salt
6 maraschino cherries
  (optional)

Cut a thin slice from the bottom of each grapefruit half so that it sits flat. Squeeze grapefruit halves, reserving 3 cups pulp and juice. Gently remove membrane, leaving shells intact; scallop edges, if desired. Freeze shells.

Combine sugar and water in a heavy saucepan. Cook over medium heat, stirring frequently, until mixture comes to a boil and sugar dissolves. Cook, stirring frequently, until mixture reaches soft ball stage (240°). Set aside.

Combine egg whites (at room temperature), cream of tartar, and salt in a large metal mixing bowl; beat until stiff peaks form. Slowly pour hot syrup in a thin stream over egg whites while beating at medium speed of an electric mixer. Turn mixer to high speed, and continue beating 5 minutes or until stiff. Add reserved 3 cups grapefruit pulp and juice, stirring well. Freeze mixture 4 hours.

Remove from freezer, and stir grapefruit mixture until well blended. Repeat freezing procedure until mixture reaches the consistency of a sherbet. Spoon into prepared grapefruit shells. Freeze until firm.

Remove from freezer 15 minutes before serving. Place on individual serving plates; garnish each with a cherry, if desired. Yield: 6 servings.

Grape Sherbet is a taste of summer, no matter when it is served.

Photographer: John O'Hagan

The fresh peach taste of Peach Sherbet is a summer delight.

LIME SHERBET

½ teaspoon unflavored gelatin
1 tablespoon cold water
2 cups boiling water
¾ cup sugar
⅓ cup fresh lime juice
Pinch of salt
Green food coloring (optional)
1 egg white

Soften gelatin in cold water. Combine boiling water and sugar in a heavy saucepan; boil 5 minutes. Remove from heat; add lime juice, salt, and softened gelatin, stirring until gelatin dissolves. Add green food coloring, if desired. Let cool.

Beat egg white (at room temperature) until stiff but not dry. Fold into gelatin mixture. Spoon into a 2-cup metal ice tray (with divider removed). Freeze until mixture becomes slushy. Remove from freezer; stir well.

Return to freezer; freeze until mixture reaches the consistency of a sherbet. Scoop into sherbet dishes, and serve immediately. Yield: 1 pint.

PEACH SHERBET

4 cups pureed peaches (about 10 large)
1½ cups sugar
Pulp and juice of 2 medium lemons
Pulp and juice of 1 medium orange
1 quart water
1 egg white

Combine peaches, sugar, lemon pulp and juice, orange pulp and juice, and water in a large mixing bowl, stirring until sugar dissolves.

Pour mixture into freezer can of a 1-gallon hand-turned or electric freezer. Freeze according to manufacturer's instructions 15 minutes or until mixture thickens.

Beat egg white (at room temperature) until stiff peaks form; fold into peach mixture. Continue to freeze according to manufacturer's instructions. Let ripen at least 1 hour before serving. Scoop into sherbet dishes, and serve immediately. Yield: about 3 quarts.

ORANGE CREAM SHERBET

1 teaspoon unflavored gelatin
¼ cup cold water
¾ cup boiling water
1 cup sugar, divided
2 tablespoons grated orange rind
¾ cup orange juice
½ cup lemon juice
Pinch of salt
1 cup whipping cream
2 eggs, separated

Soften gelatin in cold water in a large mixing bowl 5 minutes. Add boiling water and ¾ cup sugar, stirring until gelatin and sugar dissolve. Stir in orange rind, orange juice, lemon juice, and salt. Freeze until slushy, stirring occasionally.

Beat whipping cream in a medium mixing bowl until frothy. Gradually add remaining sugar, beating until soft peaks form. Set aside.

Beat egg yolks in a small bowl until thick and lemon colored. Beat egg whites (at room temperature) until soft peaks form. Fold egg whites into yolks. Fold egg mixture into whipped cream. Fold into orange mixture. Spoon into three 2-cup metal ice trays (with dividers removed). Freeze until firm.

Cut into squares or scoop out with ice cream scoop, and place in sherbet dishes. Yield: 1½ quarts.

BUTTERMILK SHERBET

2 teaspoons unflavored
  gelatin
½ cup cold water
1 quart buttermilk
1½ cups sugar
2½ teaspoons vanilla
  extract

Dissolve gelatin in cold water; set aside. Combine buttermilk and sugar in a large saucepan. Cook over low heat, stirring constantly, until sugar dissolves and buttermilk is thoroughly heated. Remove from heat; stir in dissolved gelatin and vanilla.

Pour buttermilk mixture into freezer can of a 2-quart hand-turned or electric freezer. Freeze according to manufacturer's instructions. Let ripen at least 1½ hours before serving. Scoop into sherbet dishes, and serve immediately. Yield: about 1½ quarts.

PINEAPPLE BUTTERMILK SHERBET

2 cups buttermilk
½ cup sugar
1 (8-ounce) can crushed
  pineapple, drained
1 egg white
1½ teaspoons vanilla
  extract

Combine buttermilk, sugar, and pineapple in a large mixing bowl, stirring well. Pour mixture into two 2-cup metal ice trays (with dividers removed); freeze several hours or until slushy. Remove from freezer.

Place mixture in a large mixing bowl. Add egg white and vanilla, beating well. Return mixture to ice trays; freeze until firm. Cut into squares or scoop out with ice cream scoop, and place in sherbet dishes. Yield: about 1 quart.

VANILLA ICE CREAM

9 egg yolks
3 cups milk
1½ cups sugar
¼ teaspoon salt
3 cups whipping cream
3 tablespoons vanilla extract

Beat egg yolks in top of a double boiler until frothy. Gradually add milk, beating constantly. Stir in sugar and salt. Cook over boiling water until mixture thickens and coats a metal spoon. Remove from heat, and cool completely. Chill until ready to freeze.

Pour mixture into freezer can of a 1-gallon hand-turned or electric freezer. Stir in whipping cream and vanilla. Freeze according to manufacturer's instructions. Let ripen at least 1 hour before serving. Scoop into individual bowls, and serve. Yield: about 3 quarts.

Cheerful carhop and customers at Albright and Wood Drug Store, Mobile, Alabama, 1930.

Collins Pharmacy, like most pharmacies in the early 1900s, featured an ice cream soda bar.

NO-COOK VANILLA ICE CREAM

4 eggs
2 cups sugar
1 quart plus 1 cup whipping cream
3 cups milk
3 tablespoons vanilla extract
⅛ teaspoon salt

Beat eggs in a large bowl at medium speed of an electric mixer until frothy. Gradually add sugar; beat well. Add remaining ingredients; mix well.

Pour mixture into freezer can of a 5-quart hand-turned or electric freezer; freeze according to manufacturer's instructions. Let ripen at least 1 hour before serving. Scoop into individual bowls. Yield: about 1 gallon.

EASY VANILLA ICE CREAM

¼ cup sugar
¼ cup milk
2½ teaspoons vanilla extract
⅛ teaspoon salt
1 cup whipping cream, whipped

Combine sugar, milk, vanilla, and salt in a medium mixing bowl; mix well. Slowly fold in whipped cream. Pour mixture into a 2-cup metal ice tray (with divider removed). Place in freezer for several hours or until ice cream is firm.

Cut into squares or scoop out with an ice cream scoop, and place in individual bowls. Yield: 1½ quarts.

A chilled half cantaloupe with a large scoop of vanilla ice cream makes a lovely dessert. So far as is known, the combination was first served to Lillian Russell, the famous singer-actress of the Gay Nineties. Enjoy trivia? The occasion was dinner at the Waldorf-Astoria; she was the guest of the flashy financier, Diamond Jim Brady. Unable to decide between the melon and the ice cream, she ordered both; a gallant maître d'hôtel combined the two. Voilà, a new dessert!

FROZEN CUSTARD

2¾ cups sugar
2 tablespoons all-purpose
  flour
¼ teaspoon salt
2 quarts plus 2½ cups milk,
  scalded
6 eggs, beaten
1 tablespoon vanilla
  extract

Combine sugar, flour, and salt in a large Dutch oven; gradually stir in scalded milk. Cook over medium heat, stirring constantly with a metal spoon, 15 minutes or until thickened.

Stir one-fourth of hot milk mixture into beaten eggs; add to remaining hot milk mixture, stirring constantly. Cook 2 minutes or until mixture coats the spoon; remove from heat, and cool. Stir in vanilla. Chill.

Pour custard into freezer can of a 5-quart hand-turned or electric freezer. Freeze according to manufacturer's instructions. Let ripen at least 1 hour before serving. Scoop into individual bowls, and serve immediately. Yield: about 5 quarts.

HANNAH GLASSE'S APRICOT ICE CREAM

12 ripe fresh apricots, peeled,
   seeded, and sliced
¾ cup sugar
2 cups whipping cream,
  scalded

Place sliced apricots in a heavy saucepan; cook over medium heat until bubbly, stirring constantly. Stir in sugar. Place mixture in container of an electric blender; process until smooth. Transfer to a medium mixing bowl, and stir in scalded whipping cream. Cool mixture completely.

Freeze several hours or until slushy, stirring occasionally. Remove from freezer, and pour mixture into a 1-quart mold. Freeze until firm or overnight. Unmold onto a chilled serving dish. Slice and serve. Yield: about 1 quart.

BUTTER PECAN ICE CREAM

¾ cup chopped pecans
⅛ teaspoon salt
3 tablespoons butter
½ cup firmly packed brown
  sugar
¼ cup sugar
2 tablespoons cornstarch
⅓ cup corn syrup
2 eggs, lightly beaten
2½ cups milk
1 cup half-and-half
2 teaspoons vanilla extract

Place pecans in a single layer in a shallow baking dish; sprinkle with salt, and dot with butter. Bake at 350° for 5 minutes. Remove from oven, and toss lightly. Return to oven, and bake an additional 5 minutes. Set aside to cool.

Combine sugar, cornstarch, syrup, and eggs in top of a double boiler. Gradually add milk, stirring until well blended. Place over boiling water and cook, stirring constantly, until mixture thickens. Remove from heat, and cool to room temperature; chill thoroughly. Stir in half-and-half, vanilla, and reserved pecans.

Pour mixture into freezer can of a 2-quart hand-turned or electric freezer. Freeze according to manufacturer's instructions. Let ice cream ripen at least 1 hour before serving. Spoon into individual bowls or parfait glasses, and serve immediately. Yield: about 2 quarts.

For Butter Pecan Ice Cream, the nuts are cooked in butter.

The Gem Freezer, c.1890, used elf power to make ice cream.

W hat we term double cream, standing 24 hours, is best. This sweetened and flavored gives the justly renowned Philadelphia Ice-cream, having a cream-white tint and a full rich flavor. Cooking the cream . . . prevents any tendency to curdling if cream should accidentally not be perfectly fresh, caused by very hot sultry weather. . . . When eggs are added to the cream before freezing, it is known as Neapolitan Ice-cream. . . . "

The New Dixie Cook-Book, 1895.

CHOCOLATE ICE CREAM

2 (1-ounce) squares unsweetened chocolate, melted
1½ quarts milk, scalded
4 eggs, beaten
1½ cups sugar
1 (14-ounce) can sweetened condensed milk
1 (13-ounce) can evaporated milk
1 tablespoon vanilla extract

Combine chocolate and milk in a medium mixing bowl, mixing well.

Combine eggs and sugar in a large mixing bowl; stir well. Add chocolate mixture and remaining ingredients, stirring well. Pour mixture into freezer can of a 1-gallon hand-turned or electric freezer. Freeze according to manufacturer's instructions. Let ripen 1½ to 2 hours before serving. Scoop into individual bowls, and serve immediately. Yield: about 1 gallon.

COFFEE ICE CREAM

3 cups strong coffee
¼ cup sugar
1 (10-ounce) package large marshmallows, cut into quarters
2 cups whipping cream
1 cup half-and-half
1 teaspoon vanilla extract
¼ teaspoon salt

Combine coffee, sugar, and marshmallows in a 1½-quart saucepan; cook over medium heat, stirring constantly, until marshmallows melt and mixture is well blended. Chill.

Combine coffee mixture, whipping cream, half-and-half, vanilla, and salt in a large mixing bowl, stirring until well blended. Pour mixture into freezer can of a 1-gallon hand-turned or electric freezer. Freeze according to manufacturer's instructions. Let ripen 1½ to 2 hours before serving. Scoop into individual bowls, and serve immediately. Yield: about 1 gallon.

CARAMEL ICE CREAM

2 eggs, beaten
⅓ cup all-purpose flour
2 cups milk, scalded
2 cups sugar
1 quart whipping cream

Combine eggs, flour, and milk in top of a double boiler; beat until well blended. Place over boiling water and cook, stirring constantly with a metal spoon, until mixture thickens and coats the spoon. Remove from heat, and keep warm.

Sprinkle sugar evenly in a 10-inch cast-iron skillet; place over medium-low heat. Cook, stirring constantly with a wooden spoon, until sugar melts and becomes light golden brown. Reduce heat to low, and stir one-fourth of warm custard into caramelized sugar. Continue to cook over low heat, stirring constantly, until mixture is well blended and free of lumps.

Gradually pour caramelized sugar mixture into remaining hot custard, beating constantly with a wire whisk. Cook custard mixture over boiling water until well blended and slightly thickened. Remove from heat; cool to room temperature. Chill.

Pour mixture into freezer can of a 1-gallon hand-turned or electric freezer. Stir in whipping cream. Freeze according to manufacturer's instructions. Let ripen at least 1 hour before serving. Scoop into individual bowls, and serve immediately. Yield: about 3 quarts.

An illustration from a Borden Ice Cream recipe booklet, c.1900.

Electric ice cream freezers were available in the 1920s: Surprise!

FRESH PEACH ICE CREAM

4 cups mashed peaches
   (about 8 large)
½ cup sugar
1 quart milk
1 quart half-and-half
10 eggs, beaten
2 cups sugar
1½ tablespoons cornstarch
½ teaspoon salt
2 teaspoons vanilla extract

Combine peaches and ½ cup sugar in a small mixing bowl; stir well, and set aside.

Scald milk and half-and-half in a 3-quart saucepan. Combine eggs, 2 cups sugar, cornstarch, and salt. Stir ¼ cup hot milk mixture into egg mixture; add to remaining hot milk mixture, stirring constantly with a metal spoon. Cook over medium heat, stirring constantly, 15 minutes or until mixture coats the spoon. Remove mixture from heat, and cool.

Stir in reserved peaches and vanilla; chill 2 hours or overnight. Pour mixture into freezer can of a 1-gallon hand-turned or electric freezer. Freeze according to manufacturer's instructions. Let ripen 1½ to 2 hours before serving. Spoon into individual bowls, and serve immediately. Yield: about 1 gallon.

PEPPERMINT ICE CREAM

½ pound peppermint candy, crushed
2 cups milk
2 egg whites
2 cups whipping cream, whipped

Soak crushed peppermint candy in milk in a large metal mixing bowl overnight.

Beat egg whites (at room temperature) until stiff peaks form. Slowly fold egg whites and whipped cream into candy-milk mixture. Freeze 2 hours. Beat with an electric mixer until mixture is slushy. Return ice cream to freezer for several hours or until firm.

Spoon into individual bowls, and serve immediately. Yield: about 2 quarts.

TUTTI-FRUTTI ICE CREAM

1 envelope unflavored gelatin
½ cup cold water
1 cup milk, scalded
3 cups cold milk
2 cups whipping cream
2 cups sugar
1 cup finely chopped pecans
1 cup red candied cherries, finely chopped
½ cup green candied cherries, finely chopped
6 almond macaroons, crushed
1 tablespoon strawberry preserves
1 teaspoon vanilla extract
¼ teaspoon almond extract

Soften gelatin in cold water in a large mixing bowl. Add hot milk, stirring until gelatin dissolves. Add remaining ingredients, stirring well.

Pour mixture into freezer can of a 1-gallon hand-turned or electric freezer. Freeze according to manufacturer's instructions. Let ripen at least 1 hour before serving. Scoop into serving bowls, and serve immediately. Yield: about 3 quarts.

STRAWBERRY ICE CREAM

1 quart fresh strawberries, washed, hulled, and sliced
1¾ cups sugar, divided
¼ cup cornstarch
¼ teaspoon salt
2 quarts milk
3 eggs
3 egg yolks
2½ tablespoons vanilla extract

Mash strawberries with ¼ cup sugar; cover and chill overnight.

Combine remaining sugar, cornstarch, and salt in a large Dutch oven; gradually stir in milk. Cook over medium heat, stirring constantly with a metal spoon, 10 minutes or until slightly thickened.

Beat 3 eggs and egg yolks. Stir one-fourth of hot milk mixture into beaten eggs; add to remaining hot milk mixture, stirring constantly. Cook over medium heat 2 minutes or until mixture coats the spoon. Cool to room temperature; chill several hours. Stir in vanilla.

Fold strawberries into chilled custard mixture; stir well. Pour mixture into freezer can of a 5-quart hand-turned or electric freezer. Freeze according to manufacturer's instructions. Let ripen 1½ to 2 hours before serving. Scoop into individual bowls, and serve immediately. Yield: about 5 quarts.

GREENGAGE PLUM ICE CREAM

1½ quarts milk
1 quart whipping cream
3 cups plum preserves
¾ cup sugar
Juice of 2 medium lemons
Pinch of salt

Combine all ingredients in freezer can of a 1-gallon hand-turned or electric freezer, stirring until well blended. Freeze according to manufacturer's instructions. Let ripen at least 1 hour before serving. Scoop into individual serving bowls, and serve. Yield: 1 gallon.

Greengage Plum Ice Cream: It's just "plum" good!

BEGIN WITH ICE CREAM

MOCHA MACAROON DESSERT

16 almond macaroons,
  divided
¼ cup rum
1 quart mocha ice cream,
  softened
1 cup whipping cream,
  whipped

Soak 14 macaroons in rum 10 minutes.

Line a 2-quart serving bowl with rum soaked macaroons. Chill thoroughly.

Spoon mocha ice cream into prepared bowl, and top with whipped cream. Crumble remaining macaroons, and sprinkle over top of dessert. Spoon into individual serving bowls; serve immediately. Yield: 12 servings.

MOCHA ICE CREAM ROLL

4 eggs
¾ cup sugar
1 teaspoon vanilla extract
½ cup all-purpose flour
⅓ cup cocoa
¼ teaspoon baking soda
¼ teaspoon salt
3 to 4 tablespoons sifted
  powdered sugar
½ gallon coffee ice cream,
  softened
Rich Chocolate Sauce
White chocolate leaves
  (optional)

Grease a 15- x 10- x 1-inch jellyroll pan with vegetable oil, and line bottom with waxed paper. Set aside.

Beat eggs in a large bowl until thick and lemon colored; gradually add sugar, beating constantly. Add vanilla; beat well.

Sift together flour, cocoa, soda, and salt. Sprinkle flour mixture over egg mixture, ¼ cup at a time; carefully fold in after each addition.

Spread batter evenly in pan. Bake at 400° for 12 minutes or

A soda jerk displays his skill, c.1939.

until cake springs back when lightly touched.

Sift powdered sugar in a 15- x 10-inch rectangle on a linen towel. When cake is done, immediately loosen from sides of pan, and turn out onto sugar. Peel off waxed paper. Trim ½ inch off edges of cake. Starting at narrow end, roll up cake and towel together; cool on a wire rack, seam side down.

Unroll cake, and remove towel; spread cake with softened ice cream, and reroll. Place in freezer 3 hours or until firm.

Place cake on wire rack; pour Rich Chocolate Sauce over cake. Return to freezer 3 hours or until firm.

Place roll on a serving dish. Garnish with white chocolate leaves, if desired. Slice and serve

on individual dishes. Yield: 10 servings.

Rich Chocolate Sauce:

3 (1-ounce) squares
  unsweetened chocolate
1½ cups sifted powdered
  sugar
½ cup whipping cream
⅛ teaspoon salt
¼ cup butter or margarine

Melt chocolate in top of a double boiler over boiling water. Add sugar, whipping cream, and salt, stirring constantly. Cook over boiling water until smooth. Add butter; cook 10 minutes, stirring occasionally, until butter melts. Serve at room temperature or cover and refrigerate until ready to use. Yield: 1½ cups.

RAINBOW ALASKA

1 pint strawberry ice cream, softened
1 pint vanilla ice cream, softened
1½ pints chocolate or pistachio ice cream, softened
⅓ cup shortening, softened
⅔ cup sugar
2 eggs
1 cup all-purpose flour
1 teaspoon baking powder
⅛ teaspoon salt
⅓ cup milk
½ teaspoon vanilla extract
5 egg whites
½ teaspoon vanilla extract
¼ teaspoon cream of tartar
⅔ cup sugar
⅓ cup flaked coconut

Line a deep 1½-quart mixing bowl (about 8 inches in diameter) with aluminum foil, leaving an overhang around the edges. Pack strawberry ice cream in bottom of bowl; freeze until firm. Pack vanilla ice cream over strawberry ice cream; freeze until firm. Pack chocolate or pistachio ice cream over vanilla ice cream; freeze until firm. Cover with foil; freeze until very firm or overnight.

Cream shortening in a medium mixing bowl; gradually add ⅔ cup sugar, beating well. Add eggs, one at time, beating well after each addition.

Combine flour, baking powder, and salt; add to creamed mixture alternately with milk, beginning and ending with flour mixture. Mix well after each addition. Stir in ½ teaspoon vanilla.

Pour batter into a greased and floured 8-inch round cakepan. Bake at 375° for 30 minutes or until a wooden pick inserted in center comes out clean. Cool in pan 10 minutes; remove layer from pan, and let cool completely on a wire rack.

Place cake on an ovenproof wooden board or serving dish. Remove bowl of ice cream from freezer. Set aside.

Beat egg whites (at room temperature), ½ teaspoon vanilla, and cream of tartar until frothy; gradually add ⅔ cup sugar, 1 tablespoon at a time, beating until stiff peaks form.

Invert ice cream onto cake layer; peel off aluminum foil. Spread meringue over entire surface, making sure edges are sealed. Sprinkle with coconut.

Bake at 500° for 2 minutes or until meringue peaks are browned. Remove from oven. Cut into wedges, and serve immediately. Yield: 10 servings.

CRÈME DE MENTHE PARFAITS

1 pint vanilla ice cream, slightly softened
Green crème de menthe
1 slice lemon

Spoon alternate layers of vanilla ice cream and crème de menthe into four 6-ounce parfait glasses, ending with crème de menthe.

Cut lemon slice into quarters. Garnish the top of each parfait with a lemon section. Yield: 4 servings.

Cool desserts straight from the Frigidaire were featured in this ad from a 1929 issue of Good Housekeeping.

The Historic New Orleans Collection, 533 Royal Street

Banana tree shows both bud and fruit on a postcard from New Orleans, c.1920.

CHERRIES JUBILEE

⅓ cup red currant jelly
1 (16-ounce) can pitted Bing
   cherries, drained
¼ cup brandy
Vanilla ice cream

Melt jelly in a flat skillet; add cherries. Cook over medium heat until bubbly; set aside, and keep warm.

Place brandy in a small long-handled pan; heat just until warm. Pour over cherries, and ignite with a long match. Baste cherries with sauce until flames die down. Serve immediately over ice cream. Yield: 4 servings.

ICE CREAM CUPS

¼ cup butter or margarine,
   softened
½ cup firmly packed brown
   sugar
2 eggs
¼ cup all-purpose flour
Pinch of salt
½ cup finely chopped pecans
1 teaspoon vanilla extract
Vanilla ice cream
Caramel Sauce (page 132)

Cream butter in a medium mixing bowl; gradually add sugar, beating well. Add eggs; beat well. Stir in flour, salt, pecans, and vanilla.

Drop batter by 2 tablespoonfuls, 3 inches apart (2 cookies on each baking sheet), onto greased and floured baking sheets.

Bake at 325° for 10 minutes or until browned. Immediately remove cookies from baking sheet, and shape over outside of eight inverted 6-ounce custard cups. Let cool. Carefully unmold pecan crisp cups from outside of each custard cup.

Place a scoop of ice cream in each cup. Top with Caramel Sauce, and serve immediately. Yield: 8 servings.

BANANAS FOSTER

2 tablespoons butter
¼ cup firmly packed brown
   sugar
2 bananas, peeled and halved
   lengthwise
Dash of ground cinnamon
¼ cup rum
2 tablespoons banana liqueur
Vanilla ice cream

Melt butter in a large flat skillet or chafing dish; add sugar, and cook over medium heat until bubbly. Add banana halves; heat 2 to 3 minutes, basting constantly with sauce. Sprinkle with cinnamon. Remove from heat, and set aside.

Place rum and liqueur in a small, long-handled pan; heat just until warm. Pour over bananas, and ignite with a long match. Baste bananas with sauce until flames die down. Serve immediately over ice cream. Yield: 2 servings.

NEIMAN-MARCUS TOASTED PECAN BALLS WITH FUDGE SAUCE

1 pint vanilla ice cream
1 cup chopped pecans,
   toasted
Fudge Sauce

Divide ice cream into four equal portions; shape each into a ball. Roll each ball in pecans until well coated. Wrap each pecan-coated ball in waxed paper; freeze until serving time.

Remove waxed paper from balls, and place balls in individual bowls. Pour Fudge Sauce over top, and serve immediately. Yield: 4 servings.

Fudge Sauce:

½ cup butter or margarine
6 (1-ounce) squares
   unsweetened chocolate
2¼ cups sifted powdered
   sugar
⅔ cup evaporated milk

Melt butter and chocolate in top of a double boiler over boiling water. Add sugar and milk; mix well. Cook 20 minutes or until sauce thickens. Remove from heat; beat until creamy. Serve hot over pecan balls. Yield: about 2¼ cups.

MILE HIGH ICE CREAM PIE

1 pint vanilla ice cream,
   softened
1 (9-inch) baked pastry
   shell
1 pint chocolate ice cream,
   softened
8 egg whites
¼ teaspoon cream of
   tartar
½ cup sugar
½ teaspoon vanilla extract
Chocolate Sauce

Spoon softened vanilla ice cream into pastry shell, spreading evenly; freeze until firm. Evenly spread softened chocolate ice cream over vanilla layer. Freeze overnight.

Combine egg whites (at room temperature) and cream of tartar in a large mixing bowl; beat until soft peaks form. Gradually add sugar, 2 tablespoons at a time, and vanilla, beating until stiff peaks form. Quickly spread meringue over frozen pie, sealing to edge. Place under broiler 1 minute or until meringue is lightly browned.

Return to freezer until serving time. Cut pie into wedges; place on individual plates, and serve with Chocolate Sauce. Yield: 1 (9-inch) pie.

Chocolate Sauce:

½ (4-ounce) package sweet
   baking chocolate
2 (1-ounce) squares
   unsweetened chocolate
½ cup sugar
½ cup whipping cream

Combine all ingredients in top of a double boiler. Place over boiling water and cook, stirring constantly, until chocolate melts and mixture is well blended. Continue to cook until sauce thickens. Remove from heat, and serve immediately over pie. Yield: about 2 cups.

Neiman-Marcus Toasted Pecan Balls with Fudge Sauce and, in background, Mile High Ice Cream Pie.

FROZEN DELIGHTS

APPLESAUCE MARLOW

1 cup unsweetened
   applesauce, sieved
¼ cup sugar
1 cup half-and-half
12 large marshmallows
Pinch of salt
1½ teaspoons lemon juice
½ cup whipping cream,
   whipped

Combine applesauce and sugar; set aside.

Combine half-and-half and marshmallows in top of a double boiler. Place over boiling water and cook, stirring constantly, until marshmallows melt and mixture is well blended. Remove from heat; let cool. Transfer mixture to a large mixing bowl; freeze until firm, but not solid.

Beat frozen mixture until smooth; add applesauce mixture, salt, and lemon juice, beating well. Freeze until firm.

Beat frozen mixture again, and fold in whipped cream. Pour into two 2-cup metal ice trays (with dividers removed). Freeze 3 hours or overnight. Spoon into individual serving bowls, and serve immediately. Yield: 8 servings.

A 1931 ad for General Electric refrigerator pictures party in progress.

Chocolate Marlow, from family of marshmallow-based desserts.

BANANA MARLOW

18 large marshmallows
½ cup boiling water
¾ cup mashed banana (about 2 medium)
2 teaspoons lemon juice
1 cup whipping cream, whipped

Combine marshmallows and boiling water in top of a double boiler. Cook over boiling water, stirring frequently, until marshmallows melt. Stir in banana and lemon juice. Cook an additional 2 minutes or until mixture is smooth and creamy. Remove from heat, and chill until slightly thickened.

Fold whipped cream into chilled mixture; spoon into two 2-cup metal ice trays (with dividers removed). Freeze until firm. Let stand 5 minutes before serving. Slice into bars or scoop out with an ice cream scoop, and serve in individual dessert dishes. Yield: 8 servings.

CHOCOLATE MARLOW

¼ cup cocoa
30 large marshmallows
1 cup milk
1 tablespoon vanilla extract
2 cups whipping cream
Additional whipped cream
Marshmallow hearts (optional)
Grated chocolate
Chocolate curls

Combine cocoa, marshmallows, and milk in top of a double boiler. Cook over boiling water, stirring constantly, until marshmallows melt and mixture is well blended. Remove from heat; add vanilla. Cool.

Beat 2 cups whipping cream in a large mixing bowl until soft peaks form. Fold cooled marshmallow mixture into whipped cream; spoon mixture into a 6-cup mold. Freeze overnight.

Unmold onto a serving platter. Garnish with whipped cream and marshmallow hearts, if desired. Sprinkle with grated chocolate and chocolate curls. Let stand 10 minutes before serving. Slice and serve on individual serving plates. Yield: 6 to 8 servings.

ORANGE MARLOW

1 cup orange juice
18 large marshmallows
1 cup whipping cream, whipped

Combine orange juice and marshmallows in a 1½-quart saucepan. Cook over medium heat, stirring frequently, until marshmallows melt and mixture is well blended. Remove from heat; let cool.

Fold whipped cream into orange juice mixture. Spoon into two 2-cup metal ice trays (with dividers removed); freeze until firm. Spoon into individual serving bowls. Yield: 6 servings.

CHOCOLATE MOUSSE

2 (1-ounce) squares
  unsweetened chocolate,
  melted
½ cup sifted powdered sugar
1 cup whipping cream
1 envelope unflavored gelatin
½ cup cold water
3 tablespoons boiling water
¾ cup sugar
1 teaspoon vanilla extract
4 cups whipping cream,
  whipped

Combine chocolate and powdered sugar in a medium saucepan; mix well. Gradually stir in 1 cup whipping cream; bring to a boil, stirring frequently. Remove from heat, and set aside.

Soften gelatin in cold water. Add boiling water; stir until gelatin dissolves. Add dissolved gelatin, sugar, and vanilla to chocolate mixture; mix well.

Transfer to a large mixing bowl. Chill until consistency of unbeaten egg whites.

Fold in whipped cream, and pour mixture into a lightly greased 12-cup mold. Freeze overnight.

Unmold onto a serving platter. Slice and serve on individual serving plates. Yield: 10 to 12 servings.

ORANGE MOUSSE

2 medium oranges
2 cups whipping cream
½ cup sugar
¾ cup orange juice, divided
1 teaspoon unflavored gelatin
¼ cup water
2 egg whites

Grate 1 teaspoon rind from oranges. Set aside. Slice oranges into thirteen ⅛-inch-thick slices; remove all rind, leaving orange slices intact. Cut each slice in half. Line bottom and sides of a 2-quart mold with orange slices; freeze.

Beat whipping cream in a large bowl until frothy; gradually add sugar, beating until stiff. Fold in orange rind and ¼ cup orange juice.

Soften gelatin in water in a small mixing bowl. Bring ½ cup orange juice to a boil; add to softened gelatin, stirring until gelatin dissolves. Let cool.

Beat egg whites (at room temperature) in a medium mixing bowl until stiff but not dry; fold in gelatin mixture.

Fold gelatin mixture into whipped cream mixture. Spoon into prepared mold, and freeze 4 hours or overnight. Unmold onto a serving platter. Let stand 15 minutes before serving. Yield: 10 to 12 servings.

An advertising foldover issued by Cadbury Chocolate, 1885.

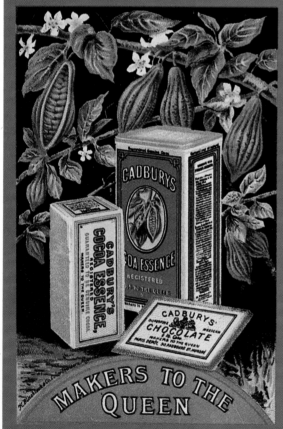

STRAWBERRY MOUSSE

1 cup butter or margarine,
  softened
3½ cups powdered sugar,
  sifted
4 eggs
1 teaspoon vanilla extract
1 (12-ounce) package vanilla
  wafers, crushed and divided
1 quart fresh strawberries,
  washed, hulled, and mashed
3 tablespoons sugar
2 cups whipping cream,
  whipped

Cream butter in a large mixing bowl; gradually add powdered sugar, beating well. Add eggs, one at a time, beating well after each addition. Add vanilla, stirring well.

Line the bottom of a 13- x 9- x 2-inch baking dish with half of vanilla wafer crumbs. Pour mixture over wafers. Set aside.

Combine strawberries and sugar in a large mixing bowl; stir well. Fold in whipped cream, and pour over top of mixture in prepared dish. Top with remaining crushed wafers. Freeze overnight.

Let stand at room temperature 15 minutes before serving. Cut into squares, and place on individual dishes. Yield: 16 to 18 servings.

Note: Strawberry Mousse may be prepared in four 2-cup metal ice trays (with dividers removed), and frozen overnight.

Collection of Business Americana

T he vanity was a popular dessert around the turn of the century. Put together with gelatin and whipped cream, it could be variously flavored, the strawberry sounding most delicious. Crushed berries were used in the mixture, and after the mold was filled, whole berries were dropped in. It was served semi-frozen, more like a bavarian or a mousse than an ice cream.

PEACH MOUSSE

1½ cups mashed, fresh ripe
  peaches (about 5 medium)
½ cup sugar
1 (13-ounce) can evaporated
  milk, chilled
1 tablespoon lemon juice
Dash of salt
Peach slices
Fresh mint leaves

Combine mashed peaches and sugar, stirring until sugar dissolves. Set aside.

Beat milk in a large mixing bowl until soft peaks form; gently fold in peach mixture, lemon juice, and salt. Spoon mixture into a 6-cup mold, and freeze overnight.

Unmold onto a serving dish. Garnish with peaches and mint leaves. Yield: 8 servings.

RASPBERRY MOUSSE

2 (10-ounce) packages frozen
  raspberries, thawed
1 cup whipping cream
⅔ cup sifted powdered sugar
⅛ teaspoon salt
Whipped cream

Process raspberries through food mill. Discard pulp; set raspberry puree aside.

Beat 1 cup whipping cream until foamy; add sugar and salt. Beat until soft peaks form. Fold in raspberry puree. Freeze 25 minutes or until firm, but not solid; beat at medium speed of an electric mixer until fluffy.

Pour into a 4-cup mold; freeze until firm. Unmold onto a serving platter. Slice, and garnish with whipped cream. Yield: 6 to 8 servings.

ANGEL PARFAIT WITH RASPBERRY SAUCE

1 cup sugar
3 cups water
3 egg whites
2 cups whipping cream
1 teaspoon vanilla extract
Raspberry Sauce

Combine sugar and water in a medium-size heavy saucepan. Cook over medium heat, stirring frequently, until mixture comes to a boil and sugar dissolves. Continue cooking, stirring frequently, until mixture reaches thread stage (230°).

Beat egg whites (at room temperature) until foamy. Pour hot syrup in a thin stream over egg whites while beating at medium speed of an electric mixer. Turn mixer to high speed; beat until stiff peaks form and mixture has cooled slightly. Cool to room temperature.

Beat whipping cream until foamy; add vanilla. Beat until soft peaks form. Gently fold whipped cream mixture into cooled egg white mixture; spoon into an 8-inch square pan. Freeze overnight.

Cut parfait into squares, and place on individual plates. Spoon Raspberry Sauce over top. Yield: 8 to 10 servings.

Raspberry Sauce:

1 cup canned raspberries, drained
¼ cup sugar

Press raspberries through a sieve using the back of a spoon. Reserve raspberry juice; discard seeds and pulp.

Combine raspberry juice and sugar in a small heavy saucepan; cook over medium heat, stirring constantly, 6 minutes or until thickened. Remove from heat; cool to room temperature. Cover; chill thoroughly before spooning over parfait or ice cream. Yield: about ½ cup.

Angel Parfait with Raspberry Sauce. For a change, spoon Raspberry Sauce around parfait.

BURNT ALMOND PARFAIT

1 cup sugar
¼ cup hot water
2 eggs, separated
1 teaspoon vanilla extract
1½ cups whipping cream
½ cup slivered almonds, toasted

Place sugar in a heavy saucepan over medium heat. Cook, stirring constantly with a wooden spoon, until sugar melts and becomes golden brown. Remove from heat; gradually add hot water, stirring constantly. Return to low heat; cook, stirring constantly, until syrup reaches thread stage (230°). Remove from heat.

Beat egg yolks; gradually pour syrup into egg yolks, beating constantly. Beat egg whites (at room temperature) in a medium mixing bowl until foamy. Gradually pour syrup mixture into egg whites, beating until cool. Chill. Stir in vanilla.

Beat whipping cream in a large bowl until soft peaks form. Fold chilled syrup mixture into whipped cream; fold in almonds. Spoon into an 8-inch square pan; freeze until firm. Scoop into individual serving dishes, and serve. Yield: 6 to 8 servings.

MAPLE PARFAIT

¾ cup maple syrup
3 egg whites
2 cups whipping cream
1 cup chopped pecans, toasted (optional)

Cook syrup over medium heat, stirring constantly, until syrup reaches thread stage (230°). Remove from heat.

Beat egg whites (at room temperature) until stiff peaks form. Pour syrup over beaten egg whites, and continue beating until mixture is cool. Chill.

Beat whipping cream in a large bowl until soft peaks form. Fold chilled syrup mixture into whipped cream. Spoon mixture into an 8-inch square pan; freeze overnight. Scoop into individual bowls, and top with toasted pecans, if desired. Yield: 8 servings.

FROZEN APRICOT LOAF

1 dozen almond macaroons
3 (17-ounce) cans apricot halves, drained and coarsely chopped
2 tablespoons lemon juice
2 cups whipping cream
½ cup sifted powdered sugar
½ teaspoon almond extract

Place macaroons on an ungreased baking sheet; bake at 325° for 25 minutes. Cool and finely crumble; set aside. Combine chopped apricots and lemon juice; set aside.

Beat whipping cream until foamy; add sugar, 1 tablespoon at a time, beating until soft peaks form. Add almond extract; beat well. Fold macaroon crumbs into whipped cream.

Alternate layers of apricot mixture and whipped cream mixture in a waxed paper-lined 9-inch loafpan, beginning and ending with apricot mixture. Freeze overnight.

Unmold onto a chilled serving platter; let stand at room temperature 10 minutes. Slice and serve on chilled dessert dishes. Yield: 8 to 10 servings.

FROZEN LEMON CUSTARD

3 eggs, separated
½ cup plus 2 tablespoons sugar, divided
¼ cup lemon juice
Pinch of salt
½ cup whipping cream, whipped
½ cup vanilla wafer crumbs, divided
Maraschino cherry halves (optional)

Beat egg yolks in top of a double boiler until thick and lemon colored. Add ½ cup sugar and lemon juice; beat well. Cook over boiling water, stirring constantly, 10 minutes or until mixture thickens. Remove from heat; set aside to cool.

Beat egg whites (at room temperature) and salt until foamy. Gradually add remaining sugar, beating until stiff peaks form. Fold meringue into cooled egg yolk mixture. Fold whipped cream into meringue mixture.

Line bottom of a 2-cup metal ice tray (with divider removed) with ¼ cup wafer crumbs. Pour prepared mixture over top, and sprinkle with remaining wafer crumbs; freeze until firm. Slice, and garnish each serving with a cherry half, if desired. Yield: 6 servings.

FROZEN LEMON DESSERT

¾ cup vanilla wafer crumbs, divided
1 (13-ounce) can evaporated milk, chilled
1 cup sugar
¼ cup plus 2 tablespoons fresh lemon juice

Sprinkle half of vanilla wafer crumbs evenly into the bottom of a buttered 9-inch square pan; and set aside.

Beat milk in a medium mixing bowl at high speed of an electric mixer until stiff peaks form. Gradually add sugar, beating well after each addition. Fold in lemon juice.

Pour lemon mixture into prepared pan; sprinkle with remaining crumbs, and freeze overnight.

Cut into squares, and serve on chilled dessert dishes. Yield: 8 to 10 servings.

FROZEN PINEAPPLE DELIGHT

1 (8-ounce) can crushed pineapple, undrained
3 eggs, separated
Dash of salt
½ cup plus 2 tablespoons sugar, divided
3 tablespoons lemon juice
1 cup whipping cream, whipped
1 cup vanilla wafer crumbs

Drain pineapple, reserving juice. Set pineapple and juice aside.

Combine egg yolks and salt in top of a double boiler; add reserved pineapple juice, ½ cup sugar, and lemon juice, stirring well with a metal spoon. Place over boiling water and cook, stirring constantly, until mixture thickens and coats the spoon. Remove from heat, and stir in crushed pineapple. Cool to room temperature.

Beat egg whites (at room temperature) in a large mixing bowl until foamy. Gradually add remaining sugar, 1 tablespoon at a time, beating until stiff peaks form. Gently fold cooled pineapple mixture and whipped cream into beaten egg whites.

Lightly butter two 2-cup metal ice trays (with dividers removed). Sprinkle the bottom and sides with vanilla wafer crumbs, reserving a small amount of crumbs for garnish. Spoon pineapple mixture evenly into each tray; sprinkle reserved vanilla wafer crumbs over top. Freeze overnight.

Let each tray stand at room temperature 5 minutes. Slice and serve on chilled dessert dishes; serve immediately. Yield: 8 servings.

BISCUIT TORTONI

1 egg white
¼ cup sugar
1 cup whipping cream, whipped
½ cup almond macaroon crumbs, divided
3 tablespoons brandy
1 tablespoon maraschino cherry juice
Additional whipped cream
8 maraschino cherries

Beat egg white (at room temperature) in a medium mixing bowl until foamy. Gradually add sugar, 1 tablespoon at a time, beating until stiff peaks form. Fold in 1 cup whipped cream and macaroon crumbs, reserving 1 tablespoon crumbs for garnish. Add 3 tablespoons brandy and cherry juice.

Place eight individual paper muffin cups in a muffin pan. Spoon mixture evenly into cups. Lightly cover with plastic wrap, and freeze until set.

Dollop each with additional whipped cream; sprinkle with reserved macaroon crumbs, and top with a cherry. Serve on individual dessert plates. Yield: 8 servings.

Caught in the Act
was the headline on this illustrated ad for the 1926 Servel refrigerator.

FROM THE DESSERT CART

In pursuit of elegance in our entertaining, we may take it into our heads to follow those social arbiters of plantation days and do a dessert table . . . not unlike today's restaurant dessert cart. Playing with a basic sketch, we center the pineapple stand or epergne (with an orange in the top dish) or a pyramid of footed glass salvers. Small figurines may be placed around it, but if we're patterning after Martha Washington, any flowers used must be artificial, lest we be thought Frenchified.

A dessert table or cart may feature almost any assortment of seductive pleasures. These must be light but rich, often harmless looking but murderously fattening. Take, for example, breezy little pastry shells, deep-fried on a timbale iron and filled with whipped cream, or cream puffs bulging with custard and draped with that menace to good intentions, chocolate.

For our baked offerings, we go from lean to fat, with Spiced Meringues and sliced Tutti-Frutti Icebox Roll marking the extremes. Meringues (kisses) have not been out of vogue since Jefferson introduced them. But our variations include tortes, some wickedly laced with cream, nuts, and dates . . . a far remove from diet food.

A word on meringue-making may be in order: When a recipe calls for chopped nuts to be added to meringue, an alarm goes off in the head of the cook who knows what grease will do to whipped egg whites. A blender or food processor tends to crush the oil from nuts, and the meringue is subsequently dragged down by the fatty content. If possible, use a Mouli grater; the nuts come out dry and fluffy. A sharp chef's knife will work well also, cutting cleanly through without squashing the nutmeats.

A dessert cart . . . or table . . . is a real live party idea. But some house specialties are designed for smaller groups, perhaps an intimate dinner party or a unique family celebration. Crêpes Suzette or Crêpes Fitzgerald are most impressive, for example, made at the table so that everyone may enjoy the conflagration.

Ready for a grand event: Dessert cart with tiered stand of fruit-topped Dessert Timbales, Chocolate Torte (left), and Tutti-Frutti Icebox Roll slices with cherry candle holders.

SPICED MERINGUES

8 egg whites
½ teaspoon cream of tartar
¼ teaspoon salt
2 cups superfine sugar
1 teaspoon vanilla extract
¼ teaspoon ground
  cardamom
Tutti-Frutti Ice Cream (page
  101)

Preheat oven to 450°.

Combine egg whites (at room temperature), cream of tartar, and salt in a large mixing bowl; beat until frothy. Add sugar, 1 tablespoon at a time, beating until stiff peaks form and sugar dissolves. Add vanilla and cardamom; beat at medium speed of an electric mixer 5 minutes.

Spoon meringue mixture into 10 equal portions on baking sheets covered with unglazed brown paper. (Do not use recycled paper.) Using back of spoon, shape meringue into circles 4 inches in diameter; shape each circle into a shell. (Sides of shells should be about 1½ inches high.)

Place baking sheets on lower rack in preheated oven; immediately turn oven off. Allow meringue to cook and cool in oven overnight. (Do not open oven door.) Carefully remove baked meringue shells from brown paper. Use immediately or store in airtight containers.

Fill meringue shells with ice cream, and place on individual dessert plates. Serve immediately. Yield: 10 servings.

Note: If desired, prepare 8 meringue shells, and pipe remaining egg white mixture into small bows. Bake shells and bows as directed. Fill meringue shells with ice cream, and garnish with bows.

Spiced Meringues filled with Tutti-Frutti Ice Cream.

PECAN MERINGUES

8 egg whites
1 teaspoon vanilla extract
Dash of salt
2 cups sugar
1 cup finely chopped pecans
Vanilla ice cream, softened

Combine egg whites (at room temperature), vanilla, and salt in a large mixing bowl; beat until frothy. Gradually add sugar, 1 tablespoon at a time, beating until stiff peaks form and sugar dissolves. (Do not underbeat mixture.) Fold in pecans.

Spoon meringue mixture into 10 equal portions on baking sheets covered with unglazed brown paper. (Do not use recycled paper.) Using the back of a spoon, shape meringue into circles 4 inches in diameter; shape each circle into a shell. (Sides should be about 1½ inches high.) Bake at 300° for 1 hour. Remove from oven, and cool away from drafts. Carefully remove baked shells from brown paper. Use immediately or store in airtight containers.

Spoon ice cream into meringue shells, and serve immediately on individual dessert dishes. Yield: 10 servings.

FRESH PEACH MERINGUES

6 egg whites
½ teaspoon cream of tartar
⅛ teaspoon salt
1 teaspoon almond extract
1 cup superfine sugar
Peach Filling
Fresh peach slices (optional)
Peach leaves (optional)

Beat egg whites (at room temperature), cream of tartar, salt, and almond extract in a large mixing bowl until foamy. Add sugar, 1 tablespoon at a time, beating until stiff peaks form and sugar dissolves. (Do not underbeat mixture.) Spoon meringue mixture into a pastry bag fitted with a star tip.

Draw 12 circles (3 inches in diameter) on 2 baking sheets covered with unglazed brown paper. (Do not use recycled paper.) Starting at center of each outlined circle, pipe meringue in a flat spiral fashion, using a circular motion that ends just inside each circle's outline. (This forms base of meringue cup.) Continue to pipe meringue atop outer ring of base, using a circular motion, to form 2 continuously attached and stacked meringue rings. (These form sides of meringue cup.) Repeat procedure with remaining meringue mixture.

Bake at 225° for 45 minutes. Turn oven off; cool meringue in oven at least 1 hour. (Do not open oven door.) Remove baked meringue cups from brown paper. Use immediately or store in airtight containers.

Place 6 baked meringue cups on individual dessert dishes. Spoon ¼ cup Peach Filling into each cup. Stack remaining baked cups, base side down, on top of filling. Spoon remaining Peach Filling evenly over top, filling cup and allowing excess to drizzle down sides. Top with fresh peach slices, and garnish plates with peach leaves, if desired. Yield: 6 servings.

Peach Filling:

2 teaspoons unflavored
  gelatin
¼ cup cold water
2 cups whipping cream,
  divided
¼ cup sifted powdered sugar
Pinch of salt
1 teaspoon vanilla extract
⅔ cup finely chopped
  peaches

Soften gelatin in cold water in a small mixing bowl. Scald ¼ cup plus 2 tablespoons whipping cream; add to softened gelatin, stirring until gelatin dissolves. Chill until mixture reaches consistency of unbeaten egg whites.

Combine remaining whipping cream, sugar, salt, and vanilla in a large mixing bowl; beat at medium speed of an electric mixer until soft peaks form. Beat chilled gelatin mixture until frothy; fold into whipped cream mixture. Gently fold in chopped peaches. Chill. Yield: about 3 cups.

Essence of summer: Child biting into a perfect peach, 1936.

SCHAUM TORTE

7 egg whites
½ teaspoon cream of tartar
¼ teaspoon salt
1¾ cups sugar
1 teaspoon vanilla extract
⅛ teaspoon almond extract
1 cup whipping cream
½ teaspoon vanilla extract
¼ cup sifted powdered sugar
1 pint fresh strawberries, washed, hulled, and halved

Preheat oven to 500°.

Combine egg whites (at room temperature), cream of tartar, and salt in a large mixing bowl; beat until foamy. Gradually add sugar, 2 tablespoons at a time, beating well after each addition. Add 1 teaspoon vanilla and almond extract; beat until stiff peaks form and sugar dissolves. (Do not underbeat mixture.)

Cover a baking sheet with unglazed brown paper. (Do not use recycled paper.) Make 25 individual meringue kisses by dropping meringue mixture by teaspoonfuls onto brown paper.

Butter the bottom of a 9-inch springform pan. Spread remaining meringue mixture evenly over bottom of pan. Place baking sheet on bottom rack of oven and springform pan on top rack. Turn oven off. Allow meringue to cook and cool in oven overnight. (Do not open oven door.) Carefully remove meringue kisses from brown paper; set aside. Loosen edge of torte with a sharp knife, and remove outer rim from springform pan. Transfer torte to a serving platter.

Beat whipping cream until foamy; add ½ teaspoon vanilla and powdered sugar, beating until soft peaks form.

Spread sweetened whipped cream over baked meringue layer. Place strawberry halves on whipped cream, and arrange meringue kisses over top. Chill. Slice into wedges, and serve on individual dessert plates. Yield: 8 to 10 servings.

Note: Baked meringue may be stored in an airtight container, and assembled the next day.

STRAWBERRY MERINGUE TORTE

2 quarts fresh whole strawberries, washed and hulled
2¼ cups sugar, divided
6 egg whites
¼ teaspoon cream of tartar
¼ teaspoon salt
¼ teaspoon vinegar
1 teaspoon vanilla extract
2 cups whipping cream, whipped

Combine whole strawberries and ¼ cup sugar in a large mixing bowl; stir gently, and chill thoroughly.

Beat egg whites (at room temperature) and cream of tartar in a large mixing bowl until foamy. Add remaining sugar, 1 tablespoon at a time, beating until stiff peaks form and sugar dissolves. Add salt, vinegar, and vanilla, beating well. (Do not underbeat mixture.)

Spoon equal portions of meringue mixture into two well-greased 9-inch cakepans. Bake at 300° for 55 minutes or until lightly browned. Remove meringue layers from pans immediately. Cool away from drafts on wire racks. Use immediately or store in airtight containers.

Place one baked meringue layer on a serving plate. Spread one-third of whipped cream evenly over meringue layer, and arrange half of whole strawberries, tapered end up, on top. Top with remaining baked meringue layer and one-third of whipped cream. Place remaining whole strawberries, tapered end up, around outer edge of baked meringue shell. Pipe remaining whipped cream in center. Chill. Slice and serve on individual serving plates. Yield: 8 to 10 servings.

Marshall's Icing Sugar displayed winning examples of icing artistry in the ad pictured in the 1894 book, Fancy Ices, *by Mrs. A.B. Marshall.*

Children's tea party, late nineteenth-century trade card.

CHOCOLATE TORTE

1 (6-ounce) package
  semisweet chocolate
  morsels
Cinnamon Meringue Shell
2 egg yolks
¼ cup water
1 cup whipping cream
¼ teaspoon ground cinnamon
¼ cup sugar
Additional whipped cream
  (optional)
Whole pecans (optional)

Melt chocolate morsels in top of a double boiler over boiling water. Cool slightly, and spread 2 tablespoons melted chocolate over bottom of Cinnamon Meringue Shell. (Chocolate layer will be thin.)

Beat egg yolks in a medium mixing bowl until thick and lemon colored. Add remaining chocolate and water, beating until thoroughly blended. Cover and chill.

Beat 1 cup whipping cream and cinnamon in a large mixing bowl until foamy; gradually add sugar, beating until soft peaks form. Spread half of spiced whipped cream evenly over chocolate layer in Cinnamon Meringue Shell. Fold remaining spiced whipped cream into chilled chocolate mixture, and carefully spread mixture over spiced whipped cream layer. Chill several hours or overnight.

Garnish with additional whipped cream and pecans, if desired. Slice into wedges, and serve on individual dessert plates. Yield: 8 servings.

Cinnamon Meringue Shell:

2 egg whites
½ teaspoon vinegar
¼ teaspoon salt
¼ teaspoon ground cinnamon
½ cup sugar

Combine egg whites (at room temperature), vinegar, salt, and cinnamon in a medium mixing bowl; beat until frothy. Gradually add sugar, 1 tablespoon at a time, beating until stiff peaks form and sugar dissolves. (Do not underbeat this mixture.)

Spoon meringue mixture onto a baking sheet covered with unglazed brown paper. (Do not use recycled paper.) Using back of spoon, shape meringue into a circle 8 inches in diameter; shape circle into a shell. (Sides of shell should be about 1¾ inches high.)

Bake at 275° for 1 hour. Turn oven off, and allow meringue to cool in oven 2 hours. (Do not open oven door.) Carefully remove Cinnamon Meringue Shell from brown paper. Use immediately, or store in an airtight container. Yield: one 8-inch meringue shell.

LEMON CREAM MERINGUE

4 eggs, separated
½ teaspoon cream of tartar
1½ cups sugar, divided
2 tablespoons grated lemon
  rind
3 tablespoons lemon juice
1½ cups whipping cream,
  divided
1 tablespoon sugar

Beat egg whites (at room temperature) and cream of tartar in a medium mixing bowl until foamy. Gradually add 1 cup sugar, 2 tablespoons at a time, beating until stiff peaks form and sugar dissolves. (Do not underbeat mixture.)

Spread meringue mixture into a lightly buttered 9-inch pieplate, covering bottom and sides. Bake at 300° for 40 minutes. Remove from oven, and cool away from drafts.

Place egg yolks in top of a double boiler; beat until thick and lemon colored. Stir in ½ cup sugar, lemon rind, and juice. Cook over boiling water, stirring constantly, 10 minutes or until very thick and smooth. Remove mixture from heat, and let cool completely.

Beat 1 cup whipping cream until soft peaks form; fold into lemon mixture. Spoon mixture into cooled meringue shell. Chill overnight.

Beat remaining whipping cream until foamy; gradually add 1 tablespoon sugar, beating until soft peaks form. Spread evenly over lemon mixture. Slice into wedges, and serve on individual dessert plates. Yield: 6 servings.

SPECIALTIES OF THE HOUSE

DESSERT TIMBALES

1 egg, beaten
1 teaspoon sugar
Pinch of salt
½ cup milk
½ cup all-purpose flour
1 teaspoon vanilla extract
Vegetable oil
Vanilla Custard
Assorted fresh fruits
Whipped cream (optional)

Combine first 4 ingredients in a medium mixing bowl; beat well. Add flour, beating until well blended; stir in vanilla.

Heat oil in a small Dutch oven to 375°. Dip timbale iron into hot oil; drain off excess oil. Dip hot iron halfway into batter; return to oil, and fry 2 to 3 minutes or until golden brown. Remove from hot oil. Gently loosen timbale from iron; drain. Repeat procedure with remaining batter.

Fill each timbale with ¼ cup Vanilla Custard; top with fresh fruit. Garnish with whipped cream, if desired. Serve immediately. Yield: about 3 dozen.

Note: If timbales are not crisp, batter is too thick; stir a small amount of milk into batter.

Vanilla Custard:

6 eggs, beaten
1½ cups sugar
½ cup all-purpose flour
4 cups milk
2 cups whipping cream
2 teaspoons vanilla extract

Combine eggs and sugar in a large Dutch oven; beat well. Add flour, stirring until smooth. Gradually stir in milk and whipping cream. Cook over medium heat, stirring constantly with a metal spoon, 40 minutes or until mixture thickens and coats the spoon. (If necessary during cooking procedure, beat mixture well with a wire whisk.) Remove from heat; stir in vanilla. Cool to room temperature; cover and chill thoroughly. Yield: about 8 cups.

CRÊPES SUZETTE

⅔ cup sugar
½ cup butter or margarine
2 orange wedges
1 lemon wedge
2 tablespoons grated orange rind
1 cup orange juice
Crêpes (recipe follows)
¼ cup brandy
2 tablespoons Bénédictine
2 tablespoons Cointreau or other orange-flavored liqueur

Combine sugar and butter in a large skillet or chafing dish; cook over medium heat until mixture is lightly browned. Add orange and lemon wedges, pressing rind with wooden spoon to extract oil. Stir in grated orange rind and juice; cook until bubbly. Remove orange and lemon wedges, and discard.

Dip both sides of crêpe in orange sauce; fold in half, and in quarters. Repeat procedure with remaining crêpes, pushing folded crêpes to side of pan.

Spoon liqueurs over crêpes in pan. Heat 1 minute without stirring. Ignite with a long-handled match. Allow flames to die down, and serve immediately. Yield: 8 servings.

Crêpes:

4 eggs
2 cups all-purpose flour
1 tablespoon sugar
1 teaspoon salt
2½ cups milk
1 teaspoon vanilla extract
Vegetable oil

Beat eggs until frothy. Combine dry ingredients; add to eggs alternately with milk, beginning and ending with flour mixture. Beat until smooth; stir in vanilla. Chill 1 hour. (This allows flour particles to swell and soften so crêpes are light in texture.)

Brush the bottom of a 6-inch crêpe pan or heavy skillet with oil; place over medium heat just until hot, not smoking.

Pour 2 tablespoons batter into pan; quickly tilt pan in all directions so batter covers bottom of pan. Cook crêpe 1 minute.

Lift edge of crêpe to test for doneness. Crêpe is ready for flipping when it can be shaken loose from pan. Flip crêpe, and cook 30 seconds. (This side is rarely more than spotty brown; fold this side to the inside.) Cool crêpe on a towel. Repeat procedure until all batter is used; stir batter occasionally. Stack crêpes between layers of waxed paper to prevent sticking. Yield: 24 (6-inch) crêpes.

CRÊPES FITZGERALD

2 (3-ounce) packages cream
   cheese, softened
¾ cup commercial sour
   cream
Basic Dessert Crêpes
½ cup butter
¾ cup sugar
3 cups fresh strawberries,
   washed, hulled, and halved
⅓ cup strawberry-flavored
   liqueur
⅓ cup kirsch or other
   cherry-flavored brandy

Beat cream cheese in a small mixing bowl until light and fluffy; stir in sour cream.

Spread 2 tablespoons cream cheese mixture evenly over each crêpe; roll up, and place two crêpes, seam side down, on 6 individual serving plates.

Melt butter in a chafing dish or heavy saucepan over medium heat. Stir in sugar, and cook, stirring occasionally, until mixture thickens. Add strawberries; cook until thoroughly heated. Set mixture aside and keep warm.

Combine strawberry liqueur and kirsch in a small saucepan; heat over medium heat. (Do not boil.) Pour over strawberry mixture, and ignite with a long match; stir until flames die down. Spoon over crêpes, and serve. Yield: 6 servings.

Crêpes Fitzgerald: A good time to perfect the flaming technique.

Basic Dessert Crêpes:

2 eggs
½ cup all-purpose flour
1 tablespoon sugar
½ cup milk
2 tablespoons water
1½ teaspoons butter or
   margarine, melted

Combine all ingredients in container of an electric blender; process 1 minute. Scrape down sides of blender container with rubber spatula; process an additional 15 seconds. Refrigerate batter 1 hour. (This allows flour particles to swell and soften so crêpes are light in texture.)

Coat the bottom of a 6-inch crêpe pan with oil; place pan over medium heat until oil is just hot, not smoking.

Pour 2 tablespoons batter into pan. Quickly tilt pan in all directions so batter covers bottom of pan. Cook crêpe 1 minute.

Lift edge of crêpe to test for doneness. Crêpe is ready for flipping when it can be shaken loose from pan. Flip crêpe, and cook 30 seconds. (This side is rarely more than spotty brown, and is the side on which the filling is placed.) Place on paper towels to cool. Stack crêpes between layers of waxed paper to prevent sticking. Repeat procedure until all batter is used, stirring batter occasionally. Yield: 12 (6-inch) crêpes.

Note: This recipe can easily be doubled.

The cook who bothers to master the technique (an easy one) of crêpe-making has a tremendous advantage when it comes to meal planning. Crêpes without sugar make beautiful first courses, with ham and asparagus rolled inside and served with Hollandaise. As a luncheon main dish, crêpes may be stuffed with innumerable good things. Most fun of all, though, is the dessert crêpe and the performance of the dramatic flambé.

CRÊPES SOUFFLÉ

4 eggs, separated
½ cup sugar
⅔ cup milk
⅓ cup half-and-half
¼ teaspoon ground mace
½ cup sifted powdered sugar
¾ teaspoon grated orange rind
8 Basic Dessert Crêpes (page 121)
2 tablespoons dark rum

Combine egg yolks, sugar, milk, half-and-half, and mace in top of a double boiler; stir with a wire whisk until well blended. Cook over boiling water, stirring constantly with a metal spoon, until mixture is slightly thickened and coats the spoon. Set aside, and keep warm.

Beat egg whites (at room temperature) until foamy. Add powdered sugar, 1 tablespoon at a time, beating until stiff peaks form. Fold in orange rind.

Divide meringue mixture into 8 equal portions, and place in the center of each crêpe. Fold crêpe in half, keeping meringue inside. Place filled crêpes in a buttered 15- x 10- x 1-inch jellyroll pan. Bake at 450° for 5 minutes.

Remove from oven; place each crêpe on a warmed serving dish. Combine reserved sauce and rum, mixing well. Spoon sauce over soufflé, and serve immediately. Yield: 8 servings.

BASIC CREAM PUFFS

1 cup water
½ cup unsalted butter
2 tablespoons sugar
½ teaspoon vanilla extract
1 cup all-purpose flour
4 eggs
1 egg white, lightly beaten
Sweetened whipped cream

Combine first 4 ingredients in a medium saucepan; bring to a boil. Add flour all at once, stirring vigorously over medium heat until mixture leaves sides of pan and forms a smooth ball. Remove mixture from heat, and cool slightly.

Add eggs, one at a time, beating well after each addition; beat until batter is smooth. Spoon batter into a pastry bag.

Line a baking sheet with unglazed brown paper. (Do not use recycled paper.) Pipe prepared batter into 3-inch mounds, 3 inches apart; lightly brush each puff with egg white. Bake at 425° for 25 minutes or until puffed and golden brown. Remove to wire racks, and cool away from drafts.

Cut tops off cream puffs; remove and discard soft dough inside. Fill cream puffs with sweetened whipped cream, using a pastry bag, if desired. Replace tops of cream puffs, and serve immediately. Yield: about 1 dozen.

Cream Puff Swan Variation:

Prepare Cream Puff Swans by following instructions for Basic Cream Puffs down through preparation of the baking sheet.

Pipe out an S-shaped neck onto unglazed brown paper, pressing out a slight bulge at one end, and tapering off quickly to a sharp point to form head and beak of swan. Brush each puff lightly with beaten egg white. Bake at 425° for 15 minutes or until golden brown. Remove to wire racks, and cool away from drafts.

Cover another baking sheet with unglazed brown paper. Pipe batter into oblong mounds about 1½ inches wide and 3 inches long to form body of swans. Brush with beaten egg white, and bake at 425° for 25 minutes or until golden brown. Remove to wire racks, and cool away from drafts.

To assemble, slice off top of cream puff body with a serrated knife; remove and discard soft dough inside. Cut top of cream puff in half lengthwise forming 2 long wings.

Fill cream puff body with sweetened whipped cream. Insert neck and wings into whipped cream to resemble a swan. Serve immediately. Yield: 10 servings.

CHOCOLATE-FILLED CREAM PUFFS DELUXE

To prepare Chocolate-Filled Cream Puffs Deluxe, follow instructions for Basic Cream Puffs down through the preparation of the batter.

Spoon batter into a pastry bag with a ½-inch plain tip. Pipe batter into 2-inch mounds, 3 inches apart, onto greased baking sheets. Lightly brush each puff with egg white. Bake at 425° for 15 minutes or until puffed and golden brown. Remove to wire racks, and cool away from drafts.

Cut tops off cream puffs; remove and discard soft dough inside. Fill bottom halves with Chocolate Pastry Cream using a pastry bag, if desired. Replace top, and sprinkle with powdered sugar. Serve immediately. Yield: 3½ dozen.

Chocolate Pastry Cream:

½ cup sugar
¼ cup cornstarch
Dash of salt
2 cups milk
4 egg yolks, lightly beaten
2 (1-ounce) squares unsweetened chocolate, melted
1½ teaspoons vanilla extract

Combine sugar, cornstarch, and salt in top of a double boiler; add milk, egg yolks, and chocolate, stirring until smooth. Cook over boiling water, stirring constantly, until mixture is very thick and smooth. Remove from heat, and stir in vanilla. Cool to room temperature. Yield: about 2½ cups.

Cream Puff family portrait taken in the Guard Room at Tryon Palace. On tray: Basic Cream Puffs and Éclairs with chocolate topping. Cream Puff Swans (rear).

ÉCLAIRS

1 cup boiling water
½ cup butter
  or margarine
1 teaspoon salt
1 cup all-purpose flour
5 eggs
Crème Pâtissière
Chocolate Butter Frosting

Combine water, butter, and salt in top of a double boiler. Cook over boiling water until butter melts. Add flour, all at once, stirring vigorously over boiling water until mixture leaves sides of pan and forms a smooth ball. Remove from heat, and cool slightly.

Add eggs, one at a time, beating well after each addition; beat until batter is smooth. (Batter will be slightly thin.) Spoon batter into a pastry bag fitted with a ½-inch plain tip.

Pipe batter into 4- x ¾-inch strips on greased baking sheets. Bake at 400° for 25 minutes. Remove from oven, and cool baked pastry completely on wire racks away from drafts.

Spoon Crème Pâtissière into pastry bag fitted with a ¼-inch plain tip. Make a small hole in both ends of baked pastry. Pipe Crème Pâtissière into one end. Frost top of each éclair with Chocolate Butter Frosting. Chill. Yield: about 2½ dozen.

Crème Pâtissière:

1 cup sugar
½ cup cornstarch
Pinch of salt
1 quart milk, divided
8 egg yolks
1 tablespoon vanilla
  extract

Combine first 3 ingredients in top of a double boiler; add ½ cup milk, and mix well. Set aside.

Scald 3 cups milk; gradually add to cornstarch mixture in top of double boiler, stirring constantly. Place over boiling water and cook, stirring constantly, until mixture is thick. Remove from heat.

Beat egg yolks in a small mixing bowl; add remaining milk. Add yolk mixture to cornstarch mixture, stirring constantly. Place over boiling water and cook, stirring constantly, until mixture is very thick. Remove from heat; let cool, stirring occasionally to prevent a crust from forming. Stir in vanilla. Yield: filling for 2½ dozen éclairs.

1901 trade card shows the sun smiling on Huyler products.

Chocolate Butter Frosting:

3 (1-ounce) squares
  unsweetened chocolate
1 tablespoon butter or
  margarine
¼ cup plus 2 tablespoons
  whipping cream
⅛ teaspoon salt
3 cups sifted powdered sugar
1½ teaspoons vanilla extract

Melt chocolate squares and butter in a heavy saucepan over low heat. Remove from heat; stir in whipping cream and salt. Gradually add sugar, stirring until well blended. Let cool; stir in vanilla. Use immediately. Yield: frosting for 2½ dozen éclairs.

KOSSUTH CAKES

½ cup butter or margarine,
  softened
¾ cup plus 2 tablespoons
  sugar, divided
2 eggs
1¾ cups sifted cake flour
1½ teaspoons baking powder
¼ teaspoon salt
½ cup milk
½ teaspoon vanilla extract
1 cup whipping cream
Chocolate Frosting

Cream butter; add ¾ cup sugar, beating until light and fluffy. Add eggs, one at a time; beat well after each addition. Combine flour, baking powder, and salt; add to creamed mixture alternately with milk, beginning and ending with flour mixture. Stir in vanilla.

Spoon batter into greased muffin tins, filling half full. Bake at 350° for 15 to 18 minutes. Cool in pans 10 minutes; remove muffins to a wire rack, and cool completely.

Beat whipping cream until foamy; gradually add remaining sugar, beating until soft peaks form. Split cupcakes in half, and spread sweetened whipped cream over bottom half. Replace top half, and frost with Chocolate Frosting. Chill until ready to serve. Yield: 1½ dozen.

Chocolate Frosting:

2 (1-ounce) squares
  unsweetened chocolate
¼ cup butter or margarine
2 cups sifted powdered sugar
2 tablespoons hot water
2 egg yolks
½ teaspoon vanilla extract
Pinch of salt

Place chocolate and butter in top of a double boiler; place over boiling water and cook, stirring constantly, until chocolate and butter melt.

Remove from heat; add sugar and hot water, beating until smooth. Add egg yolks, one at a time, beating well after each addition. Add vanilla and salt; beat until frosting reaches spreading consistency. Yield: frosting for 1½ dozen cupcakes.

OPA'S TORTE

2 cups all-purpose flour
1 teaspoon salt
¾ cup shortening
¼ cup plus 2 tablespoons
  cold water
2 (10-ounce) jars raspberry
  preserves
Whipped cream (optional)
Fresh raspberries (optional)
Fresh mint leaves (optional)

Combine flour and salt in a medium mixing bowl; cut in shortening with a pastry blender until mixture resembles coarse meal. Sprinkle cold water, 1 tablespoon at a time, evenly over surface; stir with a fork to moisten dry ingredients. Shape into a ball; chill.

Divide dough into 12 equal portions. Roll out each portion of dough on back of a lightly floured 8-inch cakepan to form a circle; prick pastry with a fork.

Bake at 450° for 8 minutes or until lightly browned. Remove pastry to a cooling rack; repeat rolling and baking procedure with remaining dough.

Spread raspberry preserves between and on top of pastry layers. Cover and let stand at room temperature 12 hours.

Garnish with whipped cream, raspberries, and mint leaves, if desired. Slice and serve on individual dessert plates. Yield: 8 servings.

Louis (Lajos) Kossuth, the Hungarian statesman and hero, before he saw America, had been active in the struggle of Hungary for independence from Austria. He fled as a political refugee to Turkey and shortly thereafter was welcomed to England as a hero. Kossuth's paper "Proclamation to the free people of the United States of North America" moved the U.S. Senate, unanimously, to provide asylum for him and his comrades. His reception in this country in 1851 was even more enthusiastic than it had been in England; he was acclaimed as a champion of freedom. When he visited Baltimore City, it is said the hospitality accorded him was exceeded only by that previously given General Lafayette in 1824. His fund-raising efforts on behalf of Hungarian independence did not come to much here, but an unknown pastry chef did create a cake in his honor: Baltimore's delectable Kossuth Cake.

New York Public Library

125

ALMOND BRITTLE TORTE

1½ cups all-purpose flour
1½ cups sugar, divided
8 eggs, separated
¼ cup cold water
1 tablespoon lemon juice
1 teaspoon vanilla extract
1 teaspoon cream of tartar
1 teaspoon salt
Almond Frosting
1 cup blanched almond
   halves, toasted

Sift together flour and ¾ cup sugar in a medium mixing bowl. Make a well in center of dry ingredients; add egg yolks, cold water, lemon juice, and vanilla. Beat at high speed of an electric mixer 5 minutes or until smooth.

Combine egg whites (at room temperature), cream of tartar, and salt in a large mixing bowl; beat at medium speed of electric mixer until soft peaks form. Add remaining sugar, 2 tablespoons at a time, and beat until stiff peaks form and sugar dissolves.

Pour yolk mixture in a thin steady stream over entire surface of egg whites, gently folding yolk mixture into egg whites.

Pour batter into an ungreased 10-inch tube pan, spreading evenly with a spatula. Carefully cut through batter with spatula, going around tube 5 to 6 times with spatula to break large air bubbles.

Bake at 350° for 50 minutes or until cake tests done. Remove from oven; invert pan, and let cool completely. Remove from pan, and cut cake crosswise into four equal layers. Spread Almond Frosting between layers and on top and sides of cooled cake. Garnish with almond halves. Yield: 12 servings.

Almond Frosting:

1½ cups plus 2 tablespoons
   sugar, divided
¼ cup light corn syrup
¼ cup hot water
¼ teaspoon instant coffee
   powder
1 tablespoon baking soda
2 cups whipping cream
2 teaspoons vanilla
   extract

Combine 1½ cups sugar, corn syrup, water, and coffee powder in a small Dutch oven. Cook over medium heat, stirring occasionally, until mixture reaches hard crack stage (300°). Remove mixture from heat; stir in soda.

Working rapidly, thinly spread mixture onto an ungreased 15- x 10- x 1-inch jellyroll pan. Let cool completely. Crush and set aside.

Beat whipping cream in a large mixing bowl until foamy; add remaining sugar and vanilla, beating until stiff peaks form and sugar dissolves. Fold prepared crushed candy into whipped cream. Yield: frosting for one 10-inch cake.

BLITZ TORTE

½ cup butter or margarine,
   softened
1¼ cups sugar, divided
4 eggs, separated
3 tablespoons milk
1 teaspoon vanilla extract
1 cup all-purpose flour
1 teaspoon baking powder
1 egg white
1 cup sliced almonds
1 tablespoon ground
   cinnamon
1 cup whipping cream,
   whipped

Grease two 8-inch cakepans with vegetable oil, and line with waxed paper. Grease waxed paper with vegetable oil. Set the cakepans aside.

Cream butter in a large mixing bowl; gradually add ½ cup sugar, beating well. Add 4 egg yolks, one at a time, beating well after each addition. Stir in milk and vanilla.

Sift together flour and baking powder. Sprinkle flour mixture over yolk mixture, ¼ cup at a time; carefully fold in. Spoon batter evenly into prepared cakepans; set aside.

Beat 5 egg whites (at room temperature) until soft peaks form. Gradually add remaining sugar, 1 tablespoon at a time, beating until stiff peaks form and sugar dissolves. Spread meringue mixture evenly over batter in prepared cakepans, sealing to edges of pans. Sprinkle top of each with sliced almonds and cinnamon.

Bake at 350° for 30 minutes. Let cool 10 minutes in cakepans away from drafts.

Invert one baked meringue layer onto cooling rack; remove waxed paper. Immediately place on a serving platter, bottom side down. Spread top of layer with one-fourth of whipped cream. Invert remaining layer onto cooling rack; remove waxed paper. Place on top of whipped cream, bottom side down. Spread sides with remaining whipped cream. Chill thoroughly. Slice and serve on individual serving plates. Yield: 8 servings.

Kellogg put out this trade card for extracts in 1890.

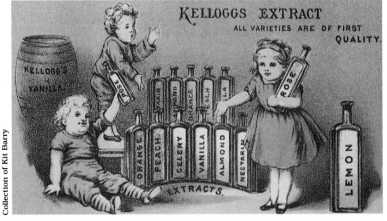

Settlers pose under Florida coconut palm, c.1890.

LEMON-COCONUT CRUNCH

1 cup grated coconut
¾ cup sugar, divided
⅔ cup graham cracker
  crumbs
¼ cup plus 2 tablespoons
  all-purpose flour
¼ cup plus 3 tablespoons
  butter or margarine,
  divided
2 tablespoons cornstarch
Pinch of salt
1 cup milk
1 egg, beaten
3 tablespoons lemon juice
½ teaspoon grated lemon
  rind
¼ teaspoon vanilla
  extract
Whipped cream (optional)

Combine coconut, ¼ cup plus 2 tablespoons sugar, graham cracker crumbs, and flour in a small mixing bowl; mix well. Melt ¼ cup plus 2 tablespoons butter in a small saucepan over low heat. Add melted butter to coconut mixture; stir well. Press half of mixture into the bottom of a lightly greased 8-inch square pan. Set remaining crumb mixture aside.

Combine remaining sugar, cornstarch, and salt in top of a double boiler; stir in milk. Place over boiling water; cook, stirring constantly, until mixture thickens. Remove from heat.

Combine egg and lemon juice in a medium mixing bowl. Gradually stir one-fourth of hot mixture into egg mixture; add to remaining hot mixture, stirring constantly. Place over boiling water and cook, stirring constantly, an additional 2 minutes. Remove from heat, and stir in remaining butter, lemon rind, and vanilla. Stir until butter melts; cool.

Pour lemon mixture in prepared graham cracker crust; sprinkle with remaining crumb mixture. Bake at 400° for 30 minutes or until golden brown. Cool completely. Cut into squares, and serve with whipped cream, if desired. Yield: 6 servings.

COCONUT CRUNCH TORTE

1 cup graham cracker crumbs
½ cup chopped pecans
½ cup shredded coconut
4 egg whites
1 teaspoon vanilla extract
¼ teaspoon salt
1 cup sugar
Vanilla ice cream

Combine graham cracker crumbs, pecans, and coconut in a medium mixing bowl; mix well, and set aside.

Combine egg whites (at room temperature), vanilla, and salt in a large mixing bowl; beat until soft peaks form. Add sugar, 1 tablespoon at a time, beating until stiff peaks form and sugar dissolves. Fold in reserved graham cracker mixture.

Spoon mixture into a well-greased 9-inch pieplate. Bake at 350° for 30 minutes or until top of torte falls and becomes crusty. Cool completely. Cut into wedges. Serve on individual dessert dishes. Top with a scoop of ice cream. Yield: 8 servings.

The cream separator was a labor-saving invention of the late 1800s.

WYATT'S PECAN DELIGHT

4 egg whites
1 cup sugar
1¾ teaspoons baking powder
¼ teaspoon vanilla extract
2 cups coarsely crushed
    saltine crackers
¾ cup chopped pecans
1½ cups whipping cream,
    whipped
¼ cup chopped pecans,
    toasted

Beat egg whites (at room temperature) in a large mixing bowl until soft peaks form. Gradually add sugar, 1 tablespoon at a time, beating until stiff peaks form and sugar dissolves. Add baking powder and vanilla, mixing well. Fold in crackers and ¾ cup chopped pecans. Pour mixture into a well-greased 9-inch piepan. Bake at 325° for 1 hour.

Remove from oven, and invert pan onto a serving platter. Cool 40 minutes; remove pan. Top with whipped cream and toasted pecans. Cut into wedges to serve. Yield: 8 servings.

Wyatt's Cafeteria had its beginnings in 1931 when the late Earle Wyatt began serving food in his grocery store on Elm Street in Dallas. The menu was simple and to the point: Cheap, nourishing, and delicious. Cornbread with beans went for a dime; barbecue sandwiches for a nickel, six for a quarter. Cafeterias are apparently a Southern phenomenon; few exist in the North. And they just happened to get into gear during the Great Depression. Britling's opened in Nashville in 1928 and the same family opened the Blue Boar in Louisville in 1931, adding the B&W in Nashville a bit later.

BEST-EVER CHEESECAKE

2 cups graham cracker
    crumbs
2 tablespoons sugar
½ cup butter or margarine,
    melted
4 (8-ounce) packages cream
    cheese, softened
1¾ cups sugar
7 eggs
3 (8-ounce) cartons
    commercial sour cream
1 tablespoon plus 1 teaspoon
    vanilla extract

Combine first 3 ingredients, mixing well. Firmly press mixture into bottom of a greased 9-inch springform pan, and chill thoroughly.

Beat cream cheese with an electric mixer in a large mixing bowl until light and fluffy; gradually add 1¾ cups sugar, mixing well. Add eggs, one at a time, beating well after each addition. Stir in sour cream and vanilla; mix well.

Pour mixture into pan. Bake at 350° for 1 hour and 5 minutes. Turn oven off. Allow cheesecake to cool in oven 4 hours. (Do not open oven door.) Remove from oven. Loosely cover; refrigerate 12 hours. Remove sides from springform pan; transfer cheesecake to a serving platter. Cut into wedges; serve on chilled dessert dishes. Yield: 12 to 16 servings.

PUMPKIN-PRALINE TART

½ cup sugar
1 tablespoon all-purpose flour
½ teaspoon salt
1 teaspoon ground ginger
1 teaspoon ground cinnamon
¼ teaspoon ground nutmeg
⅛ teaspoon ground cloves
¼ cup butter or margarine, melted
1 (16-ounce) can pumpkin
½ cup molasses
3 eggs
1 cup evaporated milk
1 (9-inch) unbaked tart shell (2 inches deep)
¼ cup firmly packed brown sugar
2 tablespoons butter or margarine
½ cup chopped pecans
1 cup whipping cream, whipped

Combine sugar, flour, salt, and spices in a large mixing bowl; stir well. Add ¼ cup butter, pumpkin, and molasses, beating well. Add eggs, one at a time, beating well after each addition. Stir in milk. Pour mixture into tart shell.

Bake at 350° for 1 hour and 10 minutes. Cool to room temperature. Chill.

Combine brown sugar and 2 tablespoons butter in a small skillet. Cook over medium heat until bubbly. Add pecans; cook an additional 2 minutes, stirring constantly. Remove from heat, and pour mixture onto a sheet of aluminum foil. Cool. Break into pieces.

Garnish tart with whipped cream; sprinkle with praline mixture before serving. Serve cold. Yield: one 9-inch tart.

Tutti-Frutti is used in the names of many desserts in which several fruits are combined. The icebox roll with this title goes back to a Texas ranch where Grace Woodruff Cartwright made it her specialty for more than fifty years. For birthdays, she used whole red cherries as candleholders, standing them in firmly whipped cream.

TUTTI-FRUTTI ICEBOX ROLL

1 (16-ounce) box graham crackers, crushed fine and divided
32 large marshmallows, cut into small pieces
1 (8-ounce) package chopped dates
18 red maraschino cherries, drained and chopped
1 cup half-and-half
1 cup chopped pecans
Additional whipped cream
12 red maraschino cherries, drained

Combine graham cracker crumbs, reserving ½ cup, marshmallow pieces, dates, chopped cherries, half-and-half, and pecans in a large mixing bowl. Mix well.

Spoon mixture onto waxed paper, shaping into a 12- x 3-inch roll. Cover with reserved graham cracker crumbs. Wrap securely in waxed paper, and chill several hours or overnight.

Cut roll into twelve 1-inch-thick slices; place each slice on a dessert plate. Dollop with additional whipped cream, and garnish with a cherry. Yield: 12 servings.

Pumpkin-Praline Tart, with a spicy filling and a crown of whipped cream sprinkled with pecan praline bits.

TOPPING IT OFF

Dessert is ready; it has been chilled or frozen or baked since yesterday and now awaits presentation. And we have our ways of getting the most out of that delectable creation. To be sure, gilding lilies is against nature, but what's to prevent our selecting the proper vase in which to arrange them, or placing them in a certain light or before a mirror to add to their impact?

Toppings, garnishes, sauces . . . these are the touches that give the finest desserts pizzazz! Here are the fudges, hot and cold, with or without a dash of spirits. Here, too, the caramel and butterscotch, the cooked and uncooked sauces of fruits and berries. Custard and other old-timers such as lemon and orange sauce have not lost their magic; they still can lift a simple pudding to awe-inspiring heights.

Let's consider whipped cream, the topping we use most often, and the problem of its watering out or separating. To avoid choosing between a dessert ruined with seepage and a last-minute dash to whip cream between dinner and dessert, here are measures we can take: In a measuring cup, soften a teaspoon of gelatin in two tablespoons milk; then place the cup in one-inch hot water, stirring until gelatin melts. While it cools a bit, start whipping cream. When it reaches the chantilly stage (i.e. soft, not firm peaks), tip in the gelatin and whip until it holds shape. A teaspoon of cornstarch cooked in two tablespoons of milk just until transparent, and added exactly the same way, is an alternate stabilizer. Either cream may be piped onto a dessert immediately or refrigerated with some confidence that it will hold.

To hold cream separately for a few hours, whip it to chantilly stage. Position a linen towel over a second bowl, securing it with a rubber band. Form the towel into a bag shape, not touching the bottom of the bowl. Turn the whipped cream out into the cloth-lined bowl, and refrigerate; the whey will drain, leaving firm cream atop the cloth.

For a change in garnishing, ladle berry puree onto the dessert plate, and set a cream puff or meringue shell in the puddle, topping off with a rosette of whipped cream. Nice!

The multi-topped banana split is only one of the ice cream parlor treats we can make at home. Sauces are, from left, Chocolate, Fresh Strawberry, and Caramel.

ALL-OCCASION SAUCES

HIGH HAMPTON BUTTERSCOTCH SAUCE

½ cup firmly packed light
    brown sugar
⅓ cup light corn syrup
2 tablespoons butter or
    margarine
⅛ teaspoon salt
½ cup whipping
    cream

Combine brown sugar, corn syrup, butter, and salt in a heavy saucepan. Bring to a boil; reduce heat and cook, stirring constantly, until mixture reaches soft ball stage (234°). Remove mixture from heat, and cool 5 minutes. Stir in whipping cream, mixing well. Serve sauce warm or chilled over ice cream. Yield: ¾ cup.

FRANCES VIRGINIA TEA ROOM BUTTERSCOTCH SAUCE

1 cup firmly packed light
    brown sugar
½ cup butter or margarine
¾ cup evaporated milk
Pinch of salt
Pinch of baking soda

Combine brown sugar and butter in top of a double boiler; place over boiling water and cook, stirring frequently, until butter melts. Add evaporated milk, salt, and soda; stir until well blended. Continue cooking over boiling water, stirring frequently, until sugar dissolves and sauce is thoroughly heated. Serve sauce warm over ice cream. Yield: 2 cups.

CARAMEL SAUCE

2 cups sugar
1 cup butter
¾ cup whipping cream
¼ cup milk

Sprinkle sugar into a 10-inch cast-iron skillet. Cook over medium heat, stirring constantly with a wooden spoon, until sugar melts and turns light brown. Remove from heat; add butter. Stir until butter melts.

Return to low heat and cook, stirring constantly, until mixture is well blended. Combine whipping cream and milk. Add whipping cream mixture to hot sugar mixture, 1 tablespoon at a time, stirring constantly, 25 minutes or until mixture is smooth and creamy. Serve warm over ice cream or pound cake. Yield: 2½ cups.

Butterscotch Sauce: A sweet link with the storied past of a unique place that stands monument to a unique man, South Carolina-born General Wade Hampton III. He came to his "valley of valleys" in Cashiers, North Carolina, as a boy in 1830 when his father was building his hunting lodge there. He fell in love with it as his father and grandfather had done and brought his Virginia bride there to live. In a mighty building spree, he built school, church, smokehouse, barns, antebellum kitchen, and ice houses . . . the site of one is now Number 18 green at the High Hampton Inn and Country Club. Hampton attained the rank of general in the Civil War and served as governor of South Carolina during the Reconstruction Era. Subsequent owners built the now-famous inn on the incomparable mountain site.

General Wade Hampton

Brady-Handy Collection, Library of Congress

Old-fashioned soda fountain in an oil painting by folk artist Alice Moseley, entitled: One Nickel and Two Straws Equal First Love.

Alice Moseley

CHOCOLATE SAUCE

8 (1-ounce) squares
  unsweetened chocolate
1 (13-ounce) can evaporated
  milk
2 cups sugar
2 tablespoons strong coffee
1 teaspoon vanilla extract
Dash of salt

Place chocolate in top of a double boiler; place over boiling water, and cook, stirring constantly, until chocolate melts. Add milk, sugar, coffee, vanilla, and salt, stirring until well blended. Cook over boiling water, stirring constantly with a wire whisk, until mixture is thoroughly heated and smooth. Remove from heat. Serve sauce warm or chilled over ice cream. Yield: about 3¼ cups.

HOT FUDGE SAUCE

7 (1-ounce) squares
  unsweetened chocolate
1 tablespoon butter or
  margarine
1¾ cups sugar
Pinch of salt
1 (13-ounce) can evaporated
  milk
1 teaspoon vanilla extract

Combine chocolate and butter in top of a double boiler; place over boiling water, and cook, stirring constantly, until chocolate and butter melt. Add sugar, salt, and milk. Cook, stirring constantly, until sugar dissolves and mixture is slightly thickened. Remove mixture from heat, and stir in vanilla. Serve sauce over ice cream. Yield: about 3½ cups.

Note: Sauce may be refrigerated in a covered container, and reheated in top of a double boiler.

SHERRIED
CHOCOLATE SAUCE

2 (1-ounce) squares
  unsweetened chocolate
2 tablespoons butter or
  margarine
⅔ cup sugar
½ cup evaporated milk
¼ cup sherry
1 teaspoon vanilla extract

Combine chocolate and butter in a heavy saucepan; cook over low heat, stirring frequently, until chocolate and butter melt. Add sugar and milk; continue to cook over low heat, stirring constantly, until sugar dissolves. Remove from heat; cool. Stir in sherry and vanilla. Serve warm over ice cream. Yield: 1½ cups.

PEACH SAUCE

4 medium peaches, peeled,
  pitted, and mashed
½ cup sugar
½ cup orange juice
2 teaspoons lemon juice
1 teaspoon vanilla extract

Combine peaches, sugar, and orange juice in a medium-size heavy saucepan. Bring to a boil; reduce heat to low, and simmer 15 minutes or until sauce thickens. Remove from heat; stir in lemon juice and vanilla. Cool. Serve warm or chilled over ice cream. Yield: 2 cups.

Picking currants, perhaps for a dessert sauce, late 1800s.

FRESH STRAWBERRY SAUCE

3 cups fresh strawberries, washed, hulled, and halved
⅓ cup superfine sugar
2 tablespoons apricot-flavored brandy

Place half of strawberries in container of electric blender. Puree until smooth. Repeat procedure with remaining strawberries.

Combine strawberry puree, sugar, and brandy in a large mixing bowl; stir until sugar dissolves and mixture is well blended. Chill thoroughly. Serve sauce over ice cream or pound cake. Yield: about 1⅓ cups.

Note: Sauce may be refrigerated in a covered container.

BRANDIED STRAWBERRY SAUCE

3 (10-ounce) packages frozen sliced strawberries
1 tablespoon cornstarch
½ cup red currant jelly
¼ cup brandy

Thaw strawberries; drain, reserving ½ cup juice. Reserve remaining juice for use in other recipes. Set strawberries aside.

Combine reserved juice and cornstarch in a small mixing bowl, stirring until smooth. Set aside.

Melt jelly over low heat in a heavy saucepan; add cornstarch mixture, stirring until thickened and clear. Add reserved strawberries and brandy, mixing well. Serve warm or chilled over ice cream or pound cake. Yield: 3 cups.

ORANGE-PINEAPPLE SAUCE

¼ cup butter or margarine
1½ cups sugar
⅓ cup pineapple juice
½ (6-ounce) can frozen orange juice concentrate, thawed and undiluted

Melt butter in a heavy saucepan over low heat; add remaining ingredients, stirring well. Bring to a boil; remove from heat. Serve warm over ice cream or pound cake. Yield: 1¾ cups.

Note: Sauce may be refrigerated in a covered container.

A souvenir cookbook for the Cotton States Exposition, Atlanta, 1895, has directions for a "Delightful Sauce." One-half cup butter is beaten into ½ cup sugar. Two egg yolks are beaten in, followed by a cup of boiling wine, or "if you have no wine, put ¾ cup whiskey, or you may instead use either a teaspoon of lemon or vanilla." We may mistrust such a switch.

BRANDIED FRUIT STARTER

1 (15¼-ounce) can pineapple
  chunks, drained
1 (16-ounce) can sliced
  peaches, drained
1 (16-ounce) can pear slices,
  drained
1 (10-ounce) jar maraschino
  cherries, drained
1 cup sugar
1 cup brandy

Combine all ingredients in a
large glass mixing bowl; stir
gently. Cover and let stand at
room temperature 3 weeks, stirring fruit twice a week. Serve
fruit over ice cream or pound
cake, reserving at least 1 cup of
fruit mixture to use as a starter
at all times.

To replenish starter, add 1
cup sugar and one of the first 3
ingredients every 1 to 3 weeks,
alternating fruit each time; stir
gently. Cover and let stand at
room temperature 3 days before
using. Yield: 4 cups.

TROPICAL FRUIT SAUCE

Grated rind and juice of 1
  lemon
Grated rind of 1 large
  orange
Juice of 2 large oranges
1 cup sugar
¼ cup butter or margarine
½ cup grated coconut
3 egg yolks, lightly beaten
1 egg, lightly beaten

Combine rind and juices in a
medium saucepan; add sugar,
mixing well. Bring to a boil. Add
butter and coconut; stir well,
and boil 5 minutes.

Combine egg yolks and egg in
a small bowl. Gradually stir in
one-fourth of hot fruit mixture;
add to remaining hot fruit mixture. Cook over medium heat,
stirring constantly, 3 minutes
or until thickened. Serve warm
over ice cream or pound cake.
Yield: 2 cups.

Note: Fruit sauce may be refrigerated in a covered container.

Making brandied fruit in a crock, 1919.

ESPECIALLY FOR PUDDINGS

GREENBRIER VANILLA SAUCE

2 cups whipping cream
½ cup sugar
4 egg yolks
1 tablespoon all-purpose flour
1 tablespoon vanilla extract
¼ teaspoon salt
1 cup vanilla ice cream

Combine whipping cream and sugar in a medium saucepan; stir well. Cook over medium heat just until mixture comes to a boil (180°). Remove from heat; set aside.

Combine egg yolks, flour, vanilla, and salt in a medium mixing bowl; beat well. Stir in one-third of hot whipping cream mixture; add to remaining hot whipping cream mixture, stirring well.

Cook over medium heat, stirring constantly, until slightly thickened. Remove from heat; add vanilla ice cream, and stir until ice cream melts. Serve sauce warm or chilled over pudding. Yield: 3 cups.

Creamy Lemon Sauce: A treat with Ginger Pudding.

IRMA'S EGGNOG SAUCE

3 egg yolks
3 tablespoons sugar
Pinch of salt
¼ cup plus 2 tablespoons bourbon
1 cup whipping cream
Ground nutmeg (optional)

Beat egg yolks in a medium bowl until thick and lemon colored. Gradually add sugar and salt, beating constantly. Add bourbon, beating well.

Beat whipping cream until soft peaks form. Fold whipped cream into yolk mixture. Serve over steamed pudding. Sprinkle with ground nutmeg, if desired. Yield: 3 cups.

Note: Sauce may be refrigerated in a covered container.

BOURBON SAUCE

2 tablespoons butter
1 cup firmly packed light brown sugar
⅛ teaspoon salt
2 tablespoons bourbon
1 cup whipping cream

Brown butter in a cast-iron skillet over medium heat; stir in brown sugar and salt, using a wooden spoon. Cook mixture over low heat, stirring frequently, until sugar dissolves. Add bourbon and whipping cream, stirring well. Continue cooking until sauce thickens. Serve sauce warm over pudding. Yield: about 1½ cups.

CREAMY LEMON SAUCE

¼ cup butter or margarine, softened
1 cup sugar
½ cup whipping cream
2 eggs, beaten
Grated rind and juice of 2 medium lemons

Cream butter in top of a double boiler; gradually add sugar, beating well. Add whipping cream, eggs, and lemon rind and juice, beating well. Place over boiling water and cook, stirring constantly, until mixture is smooth and glossy. Serve sauce warm over pudding. Yield: 1½ cups.

TART LEMON SAUCE

1 cup sugar
1 tablespoon plus 2
  teaspoons all-purpose flour
¼ teaspoon salt
1 cup water
1 tablespoon butter or
  margarine
1 tablespoon grated lemon
  rind
3 tablespoons lemon juice

Combine sugar, flour, and salt in a small heavy saucepan; add water, stirring until mixture is smooth. Bring mixture to a boil; cook 3 minutes, stirring frequently. Remove from heat; add butter, grated lemon rind, and lemon juice, stirring until butter melts. Serve warm over pudding or gingerbread. Yield: about 1⅔ cups.

OLD-FASHIONED GOLDEN LEMON SAUCE

½ cup butter or margarine
1 cup sugar
Grated rind and juice of 1
  lemon
¼ cup boiling water
1 egg, beaten

Melt butter in top of a double boiler over boiling water. Reduce heat to medium, and gradually stir in sugar, lemon rind and juice, and boiling water. Gradually stir 1 tablespoon of hot mixture into beaten egg; add to remaining hot mixture, stirring constantly. Cook over boiling water, stirring constantly, until thickened. Remove from heat, and serve warm over pudding. Yield: 1⅓ cups.

ORANGE SAUCE

½ cup sugar
1 tablespoon plus 2
  teaspoons cornstarch
¼ teaspoon salt
1 cup water
1 tablespoon butter or
  margarine
1 teaspoon grated orange rind
¼ cup fresh orange juice
¼ teaspoon orange extract

Combine sugar, cornstarch, salt, and water in a medium saucepan, stirring until dry ingredients dissolve. Cook over low heat, stirring constantly, until mixture is clear. Add butter, orange rind, juice, and flavoring. Continue to cook, stirring constantly, 5 minutes or until sauce thickens. Serve warm over pudding. Yield: about 1½ cups.

HARD SAUCE

¼ cup butter or margarine,
  softened
¾ cup sifted powdered sugar
1 egg white
2 teaspoons brandy

Cream butter in a small mixing bowl. Add remaining ingredients, beating until well blended. Serve over puddings. Yield: about ¾ cup.

HOT SHERRY SAUCE

1 cup butter or margarine,
  softened
1 cup sugar
1 egg yolk
½ cup sherry
Pinch of ground nutmeg

Cream butter in a medium saucepan; gradually add sugar, beating until light and fluffy. Add egg yolk, and beat well. Cook over medium heat 2 minutes or until mixture is smooth and creamy. Stir in sherry and nutmeg; cook, stirring constantly, until mixture thickens. Serve hot over pudding. Yield: 2¼ cups.

WINE SAUCE

2½ cups sifted powdered
  sugar
½ cup boiling water
2 tablespoons butter or
  margarine
¼ cup sherry
¼ cup brandy
1 teaspoon ground
  nutmeg

Combine sugar, water, and butter in a saucepan, stirring well. Bring to a boil; reduce heat and cook, stirring constantly, 3 to 4 minutes. Remove from heat; stir in remaining ingredients, mixing well. Serve warm over pudding. Yield: 2 cups.

Note: This old-fashioned dessert sauce is especially good with gingerbread.

WINE CUSTARD SAUCE

5 eggs, lightly beaten
1 cup sugar
Grated rind and juice of 1
  lemon
1 tablespoon plus 1 teaspoon
  cornstarch
2 tablespoons water
2 cups Sauterne or other
  sweet white wine

Combine eggs and sugar in top of a double boiler; beat well. Stir in lemon rind and juice. Dissolve cornstarch in water; add to egg mixture, mixing well. Stir in wine.

Place over boiling water, and cook, stirring constantly, 20 minutes or until mixture thickens. Remove from heat; cool to room temperature. Cover and refrigerate. Serve chilled over pudding. Yield: 4 cups.

ACKNOWLEDGMENTS

Almond Brittle Torte adapted from *The Woman's Club of Ft. Worth Cookbook* by members of The Woman's Club and Jr. Woman's Club of Ft. Worth, ©1955. By permission of The Woman's Club of Ft. Worth, Texas.

Apple Crumble, by Mrs. Garrett W. Judy, first appeared in *The Gasparilla Cookbook* by The Junior League of Tampa, ©1961. By permission of The Junior League of Tampa, Florida.

Apricot Fool, Brandied Nectarines, Filbert Pudding with Apricot Sauce, Greengage Plum Ice Cream, Honey Flummery adapted from *Thirteen Colonies Cookbook* by Donovan, Hatrack, Mills, and Shull. By permission of Holt, Rhinehart and Winston, New York.

Arkansas Rice Pudding, Coconut Cream with Caramel Sauce, Ozark Pudding adapted from *Prairie Harvest* by St. Peter's Episcopal Churchwomen, Tollville, Arkansas. By permission of St. Peter's Episcopal Churchwomen, Hazen, Arkansas.

Baked Coconut Cup Custard, Frances Virginia Tea Room Butterscotch Sauce, Hot Fudge Sauce, Lemon Coconut Crunch, Orange Sauce adapted from *Frances Virginia Tea Room Cookbook* by Mildred Huff Coleman, ©1982. By permission of Peachtree Publishers, Limited, Altanta.

Banana Cream Pudding, by Mrs. Robert A. Foster, first appeared in *The Gasparilla Cookbook* by The Junior League of Tampa. By permission of The Junior League of Tampa.

Bananas Foster, Caramel Custard Petit Arnaud, Crêpes Soufflé, Mile High Ice Cream Pie, Chocolate Mousse adapted from *Secrets from New Orleans' Best Kitchens* by Earlyne S. Levitas, ©1973. By permission of Secrets, Alanta, Georgia.

Biscuit Tortoni, by Mrs. E.P. Taliaferro, Jr., first appeared in *The Gasparilla Cookbook* by The Junior League of Tampa. By permission of The Junior League of Tampa.

Bishop Whipple Pudding, by Mrs. Stephen M. Sparkman, first appeared in *The Gasparilla Cookbook* by The Junior League of Tampa. By permission of The Junior League of Tampa.

Blackberry Sherbet, Cranberry Sherbet, Easy Boiled Custard adapted from *The Gardener's Cookbook*, edited by Mildred W. Schlumpf.

Blueberry Grunt adapted from *Pioneer Cookery Around Oklahoma*, compiled and edited by Linda Kennedy Rosser, ©1978. By permission of Linda Kennedy Rosser and Bobwhite Publications, Oklahoma City, Oklahoma.

Blueberry Soufflé, Hot Lemon Soufflé adapted from *Dallas Symphony League Cookbook* by the Junior Group of the Dallas Symphony Orchestra League. By permission of the Junior Group, Dallas, Texas.

Bon Ton's Bread Pudding courtesy of Bon Ton's Restaurant, New Orleans.

Bread Pudding with Wine Sauce, Opa's Torte, Wine Custard Sauce adapted from *Guten Appetit!* by The Sophienburg Museum, ©1978. By permission of The Sophienburg Museum, New Braunfels, Texas.

Buttermilk Sherbet adapted from *Harris County Heritage Society Cookbook*. By permission of The Harris County Heritage Society, Houston, Texas.

Buttermilk Sherbet and Orange Cream Sherbet courtesy of Mrs. Ed Brown, Pine Bluff, Arkansas.

Butter Pecan Ice Cream adapted from *The Nashville Cookbook* by The Nashville Area Home Economics Association. By permission of The Nashville Area Home Economics Association, Nashville, Tennessee.

Caramel Flan, Fresh Guava Cobbler, Orange-Pineapple Sauce, Strawberries à la Mode, Sweet Potato Pone, Watermelon Bowl adapted from *Jane Nickerson's Florida Cookbook*, ©1973. By permission of University Presses of Florida, Gainesville.

Caramel Sponge Pudding, Irma's Eggnog Sauce, Hot Chestnut Soufflé, Steamed Swiss Pudding with Golden Lemon Sauce adapted from *Out of Kentucky Kitchens* by Marion Flexner, ©1949. By permission of Franklin Watts, Inc., New York.

Chocolate Marlow adapted from *De Bonnes Choses à Manger* by St. Matthew's Guild, Houma, Louisiana.

Chocolate Marshmallow Dessert, by Mrs. Whitfield Palmer, first appeared in *The Gasparilla Cookbook* by The Junior League of Tampa. By permission of The Junior League of Tampa.

Coconut Crunch Torte, Peach Mousse adapted from *Favorite Recipes From The Big House* by the N.G. Davis Family, ©1981. By permission of Cookbook Publishers, Lenexa, Kansas.

Connemara Baked Custard courtesy of The Carl Sandburg Home, National Historic Site, Flat Rock, North Carolina.

Crêpes Suzette, Fresh Peach Crisp, Fried Custard adapted from *Talk About Good!* by The Junior League of Lafayette, ©1969. By permission of The Junior League of Lafayette, Louisiana.

Date Pudding with Cherry Sauce courtesy of Mrs. Clint Wyrick, Garland, Texas.

Dessert Timbales adapted from *Ozarks Cookery* by Eula Mae Stratton, ©1976. By permission of *The Ozark Mountaineer*, Branson, Missouri.

Easy Vanilla Ice Cream, No-Cook Vanilla Ice Cream, Refrigerator Cheesecake adapted from *Dear Daughter* by Eula Mae Tucker. By permission of Eula Mae Tucker, Marionville, Missouri.

Frozen Dessert courtesy of Mrs. George Welch, Columbus, Mississippi.

Grapefruit Sherbet, Texas Grapefruit Parfait, Sunrise Compote courtesy of TexaSweet Citrus Advertising, Inc., McAllen, Texas.

Grape Sherbet courtesy of Mrs. J.D. Robinson, Garland, Texas.

Greenbrier Vanilla Sauce, The Greenbrier Cold Bourbon Soufflé adapted from *Legendary Specialties from The Greenbrier*. Courtesy of The Greenbrier Hotel, White Sulphur Springs, West Virginia.

High Hampton Butterscotch Sauce courtesy of The High Hampton Inn, Cashiers, North Carolina.

Kossuth Cakes adapted from *Maryland's Way* by Mrs. Lewis R. Andrews and Mrs. J. Reaney Kelly. By permission of The Hammond-Harwood House Association, Annapolis, Maryland.

Lemon Cream Meringue adapted from *Christmas in Oklahoma*, compiled and edited by Linda Kennedy Rosser, ©1982. By permission of Linda Kennedy Rosser and Bobwhite Publications, Oklahoma City, Oklahoma.

Mango Flameador, by Miriam Fineberg, first appeared in *Delicioso!* by The Junior League of Corpus Christi, ©1982. By permission of The Junior League of Corpus Christi, Texas.

Neiman-Marcus Toasted Pecan Balls with Fudge Sauce adapted from *Neiman-Marcus — A Taste of the Past*. By permission of Neiman-Marcus, Dallas, Texas.

Norwegian Rice Pudding, Scandinavian Creamy Porridge adapted from *From Norse Kitchens* by Our Savior's Lutheran Church Women. By permission of Our Savior's Lutheran Church Women.

Orange Custard courtesy of Mrs. William David Roddey, Jr., Warren, Arkansas.

Peach Tart, Wine Jelly Mold adapted from *The Plantation Cookbook* by The Junior League of New Orleans, ©1972. By permission of Doubleday and Company, Inc., New York.

Peach Sauce adapted from *Seems Like I Done It This A-Way* by Cleo Stiles Bryan. Courtesy of Cleo Stiles Bryan, Tahlequah, Oklahoma.

Pumpkin-Praline Tart adapted from *Southern Sideboards* by The Junior League of Jackson, ©1978. By permission of The Junior League of Jackson, Mississippi.

Rose Hill Strawberries courtesy of Anne Stallworth McKeown, Jackson, Mississippi. First appeared in *Stallworth Roots and Recipes*.

Snowden House Rum Mousse courtesy of Mr. Edgar Snowden, Bethesda, Maryland.

Spiced Meringues adapted from *The Spices of the World Cookbook by McCormick*, revised edition, ©1964, 1977. Courtesy of McCormick and Company, Incorporated, Baltimore, Maryland.

Strawberries in Wine adapted from *The Melting Pot: Ethnic Cuisine in Texas* by the Institute of Texan Cultures, ©1977. By permission of The University of Texas, Institute of Texan Cultures, San Antonio, Texas.

Strawberry Meringue Torte, by Mrs. Myron Gibbons, first appeared in *The Gasparilla Cookbook* by The Junior League of Tampa. By permission of The Junior League of Tampa.

Tarboro Tipsy Cake adapted from *The Southern Cookbook* by Marion Brown, ©1951. By permission of The University of North Carolina Press, Chapel Hill, North Carolina.

Tutti-Fruitti Icebox Roll adapted from *Cartwright Cuisine* by Marilyn Mays Bloemendal, Patty Cartwright Harvey, and Mollie Lupe Lasater, ©1983. By permission of The Cartwright Family, Ft. Worth, Texas.

Wine Sauce adapted from *Norfolk Cookery* by Sandra Woodward, ©1982. By permission of Donning Company/Publishers, Norfolk, Virginia.

Woodford Pudding adapted from *Flavor Favorites* by The Baylor University Alumni, ©1979. By permission of The Baylor University Alumni Association, Waco, Texas.

Wyatt's Pecan Delight courtesy of Wyatt Cafeterias, Dallas, Texas.

Back cover art courtesy of Harris County Heritage Society.

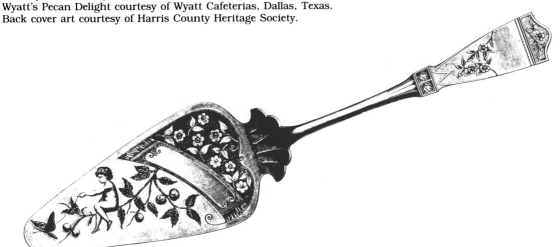

INDEX

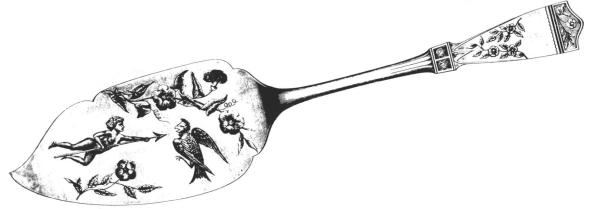

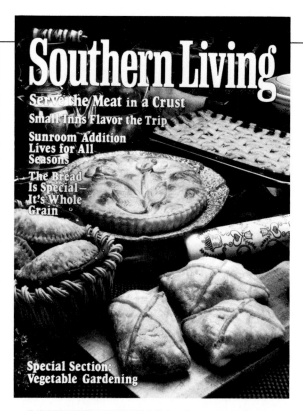